Myth-
Informed

MYTH-INFORMED

LEGENDS, CREDOS, AND WRONGHEADED "FACTS" WE ALL BELIEVE

Paul Dickson
And Joseph C. Goulden

A PERIGEE BOOK

Perigee Books
are published by
The Putnam Publishing Group
200 Madison Avenue
New York, NY 10016

Library of Congress Cataloging-in-Publication Data
Dickson, Paul.
Myth-Informed : legends, credos, and wrongheaded "facts" we all believe /
Paul Dickson and Joseph C. Goulden.
p. cm.
Includes bibliographical references and index.
ISBN 0-399-51839-8 (acid-free paper)
1. Folklore—United States. 2. Popular culture—United States. 3. United
States—Social life and customs. I. Goulden, Joseph C.
II. Title.
GR105.D527   1993   93-4135 CIP
398′.0973—dc20

Cover design and illustration © 1993 by Robert Korn
Printed in the United States of America
6   7   8   9   10

TERMS

Credo is Latin for "I believe." As an English word it originally referred to religious creeds, such as the Apostles' Creed, but then came to mean any belief or creed. Mainly due to the influence of H. L. Mencken and George Jean Nathan and their book *The American Credo*, it has taken on a new meaning in the twentieth century. Today it commonly refers to a widely held belief or piece of conventional wisdom that is partially, predominantly, or totally wrong. In this book we deal exclusively with this type of credo.

These wrongheaded credos naturally break down into two basic species. First, there are the *specific credos:* bits of silliness that must be apocryphal in origin—beliefs about reptiles in sewers and admirals being unable to navigate rowboats. Secondly, there is the *philosophical credo:* a belief with a genuine element of truth to it, but one that has become so clichéd and over-applied that it now exhibits a genuine element of falsehood. Examples: that there are two sides to every question, or that you can discipline your mind. (If you've just caught yourself saying "What? of course that's true!" you've been suckered in by another credo.) This collection concentrates on the former, but is salted with some of the latter.

The twentieth-century American credo also has a first cousin that any self-respecting credo collector cannot resist accumulating. It is the modern fable—or what folklorists call the *urban folktale*—and it is essentially a credo that has been turned into a story. The authors proudly exhibit their fable collection along with their credos.

CONTENTS

PREFACE

After H. L. Mencken

The trouble with most folks isn't so much their ignorance, as know-
ing so many things that ain't so.

—Josh Billings

Deep down in every man there is a body of congenital attitudes, a
corpus of ineradicable doctrines and ways of thinking, that deter-
mines his reactions to his ideational environment as surely as his
physical activity is determined by the length of his tibiae and the
capacity of his lungs.

—H. L. Mencken and George Jean Nathan,
The American Credo, *1920*

In 1920, satirists H. L. Mencken and George Jean Nathan pub-
lished a book called The American Credo. *It contained a chres-*
tomathy of shibboleths, prejudices, common beliefs and unexamined
truisms held sacred by millions—"That it snowed every Christmas
down to fifteen years ago," for example, or "that oysters are a great
aphrodisiac." The Credo *badly needs updating.*

—Unnamed editor, Time Magazine, *September 28, 1970.*

From the first stirrings of childhood the American acquires an
ever-thickening encrustation of ideas, beliefs, and dogmas that
make life all the simpler. Tribal truths pass to this youngster
from his elders and his contemporaries, to be assimilated into
common acceptances, an intellectual shorthand that enables
that young man or woman to pass through life with a mini-
mum of mental effort.

What, for instance, does one really need to know about
dogs save that a canine who wags his tail when barking is not
a menace? Or that the primary function of carrots is to
strengthen one's eyesight? Or that the consumption of fish
benefits the brain? Specialists in zoology, nutrition, and neurol-

ogy perhaps will seek a bit more detail; the layman cares to know no more.

That much of what passes for "knowledge" in America is rank nonsense is of no great importance. The progress of mankind is oiled by perceptions, not realities. That the general populace treats a notion as truth gives it a momentum and a life of its own. Indeed, major segments of our society survive because of this principle. What politician dares introduce a truly new idea to the electorate? Consider the Democratic party. For two decades its office seekers of any denomination, from alderman to President, merely had to bellow "Herbert Hoover" from time to time, code words that reminded the electorate of the Depression, and the person responsible for it. The Republicans, equally sharp on the rules of play, needed only to mutter "Alger Hiss" and "Who lost China?" to wiggle their way back to the front of the line.

In each of these instances the parties relied upon a "credo"—the willingness of Americans to accept a proposition as fact, without cumbersome footnotes and explanations. The credo thus has a double utility: the people who employ it need go no further than a phrase, a wink, and a nod; the people who hear it are conditioned to accept what is offered.

That Americans have been subjected to an "information explosion" in the last decade or two verily is a credo unto itself. Assuredly the quantity of information offered has increased dramatically. Satellite television transmissions permitted us to witness in our living rooms the U.S.-led air assault on Baghdad in 1990's Operation Desert Storm as it occurred. When Napoleon's army floundered in Egypt in 1798, news of the disaster did not reach Paris for months. Our newsstands offer magazines on every "specialty" from bathroom design to the techniques of placer mining. Yet how much of this available knowledge is actually assimilated? Does it have any impact upon the already accepted "truth"?

Sadly, not much. Americans might be blessed with a plethora of new information, some of which is undoubtedly absorbed. But they are equally slow to abandon old notions. When the aforementioned Messrs. Mencken and Nathan compiled their *American Credo* in 1920, they marveled that many beliefs rampant in the gin mills and dance halls of the Jazz Age had also enthralled peasants hovering around dung-heap fires in the Dark Ages. The theological baggage a 1920s bishop bore on his daily rounds was interchangeable with that of a medieval monk's, even if contained in a gaudier package.

Trolling many of the same waters seven decades later, our hooks regularly snatched up many of the credos already netted and cleaned by Mencken and Nathan. Thus we ask, Is America a Dead Sea in which ideas slosh back and forth interminably, without discernible change?

Walter Blair, a folk legend specialist who adorns the faculty of the University of Chicago, maintains that the *language* of credos might change, but seldom the *substance*. Briskly mustering his evidence, Professor Blair directs his pointer at the modern credo "Doctors often overlook illness and injury in their own families." Blair peers back two centuries, to Benjamin Franklin and his *Poor Richard's Almanack:* "There's more old drunkards than old doctors." Consider also, Blair suggests, the modern credo "Any New England farmer has more common sense than a Harvard professor." As Franklin's Poor Richard put it, "Tim was so learned, that he could name a horse in nine languages. So ignorant, that he bought a cow to ride on." In their book *America's Humor: From Poor Richard to Doonesbury,* Blair and coauthor Hamlin Hill cite numerous restatements of this concept over the centuries and conclude that "the most dependable American joke" is the "one based upon the way educated people miss the truth by using book learning while humble, unlearned people find the truth by using their horse sense." A modern variant involves the unlettered old man who earns so much money from a roadside fried-chicken stand that he is able to send his son to the Harvard business school, where he learns modern management techniques. Back home, he applies these theories to his father's business and bankrupts it within a year. The father boasts, "My son, he is so smart; had he not gone to Harvard, we would have been broke even faster."

Lest we sound overly critical of the collective popular intellect, 1990s America is due credit for advances in the distillation and distribution of credos. Centuries ago, what old women babbled one to the other in the marketplace was the generic equivalent of *The New York Times*. Given any semblance of plausibility, spoken rumor quickly hardened into truth. If people die and leave no permanent record of their minor beliefs, those credos are forgotten. But put the rumor into print, and give it the brevet rank of fact, and it is history.

Our equivalent of marketplace babble is the racks of tabloid newspapers found in supermarkets, the foremost source of nonsense in the Western world. Even for nonreaders the exposure to these newspapers has subliminal impact. One's mind dizzies at headlines about UFOs whizzing Jackie O. away to a rendezvous with the spirit of Liberace, evangelists exploding in their pulpits, Bigfoot taking brides from shopping malls, and the face of Elvis showing up on the moon through a telescope. Nuts who would be chased out of any city room in the Republic peddle yarns about green-eyed monsters and miracle cures and reincarnations of James Dean. These stories are printed without a blush, and they are read, and they are believed. And if they can't get a hearing at the tabloids then there are outrageous television shows that have become so sensational that they are now pedestrian. These are shows that would make "guest hosts" of Charles Manson or Jeffrey Dahmer if either ever gets out of jail. (Meanwhile, we'll have to settle for shows with topics like "Women Who Love Serial Killers," which aired in the spring of 1993 on the Jenny Jones syndicated talk show and could boast of two guests who had fallen in love with the afore-mentioned Dahmer.)

Why? Stated impolitely, because this nation, during the past few decades, has with good reason skittered along the brink of collective paranoia. Watergate and its congeries of zany schemes and subschemes. Vietnam, and the damage done to truth, among other things. The CIA and the FBI, under joint management of the Marx Brothers and Gilbert & Sullivan. The assassinations, and the plot-cults attendant to them. *Incredulous* survives only as a word found in the dictionary. Heaped onto this has been a rich sauce of debacle: a monstrous savings-and-loan scandal, Congressional high jinks and bounced checks, big troubles at Big Blue, a legion of special prosecutors, and so much more.

Thus we have grafted onto the homilies of the past the new nuttiness of the present. Peasants once fell prostrate at the sight of an eclipse of the sun, bellowing to the deities for salvation, convinced that a supernatural being was about to snatch them off the earth. Their lineal descendants—that is to say, we— have progressed to a belief in extraplanetary spaceships that prowl the backwoods by night, collecting herdsmen and beautiful girls, and perhaps indulging in blood sacrifices of livestock as well. That "evidence" of such happenings is skimpy is laid to "the government," which conceals "facts" lest the populace panic.

Yet this sort of nonsense does have social utility. One of the authors once listened, with marked interest, to the ideas propounded by persons who telephoned a late-night radio talk show. The subject at hand happened to be the military, and the callers advanced some most conspiratorial views of contemporary history: that General Douglas MacArthur and Marshal Georgy Zhukov, the Red Army commander, "planned" the Korean War during a secret meeting in Thailand in 1947; and that a "Russian general at the United Nations" directed overall American military strategy in the Korean War. "This is kind of far-out stuff," the author remarked to the moderator, who replied, "Yeah, but at least listening to the radio keeps them off the street. Would you rather have them running around at this time of night?" No. The offsetting mischief, however, is that a listener elsewhere hears a snatch of this gabble and stores it away as truth—because, after all, does not the Federal Communications Commission have laws against false information being disseminated over the radio?

The amount of evidence required to substantiate the validity of a credo is a free-floating variable. For example, "Bad airplane accidents always occur in threes." If there is a major airline crash, adherents to the "threes credo" keep a watch on the newspapers the following days. In all probability they'll read about a second crash in the Far West, and of another in South America. Thus the "threes credo" is substantiated. Or news of the conviction of a minister on morals charges reinforces the belief that much naughtiness is performed under the guise of theology, statistical evidence to the contrary notwithstanding.

That the modern myths have established themselves as an integral part of American folklore is recognized by no less a cultural barometer than Hollywood. During the 1960s there were murmurings from the nut fringe that the space shots and moon walks never occurred; that in actuality all these events were staged on remote sites in the Nevada desert. ("Look at any road map. See these vast areas that are marked 'military reservations'? That's where it happened.") In 1978 Hollywood put a variation of this canard onto film in *Capricorn One,* in which O. J. Simpson, Hal Holbrook, and James Brolin played bogus astronauts.

The "fake moon walk" yarn has considerable currency abroad, Michael Ledeen discovered while working as a consultant to the Reagan Administration. Talking with a top officer of the Khomeini regime in Iran in 1985, Ledeen was surprised to hear the man say, "We know how tricky Americans can be. That story about landing on the moon, for example. We know that never happened, that it was all propaganda. . . ." A few weeks later a friend in Soweto, South Africa, assured Ledeen the landing never happened: "all propaganda, all Hollywood." Then Soviet General Ivan Yershov, who commanded the 1968 invasion of Czechoslovakia, visited the Air and Space Museum in Washington and looked with fascination at the moon rocks. "So it was true all along," he told Ledeen with amazement. Recounting his experiences in *The Wall Street Journal* on January 23, 1990, Ledeen concluded "that much of the world is deeply skeptical of the stuff that appears on American television."

Capricorn One, which set the "fake moon walk" story in the popular mind, was quickly followed by *The Formula,* with George C. Scott and Marlon Brando feuding over the secret to cheap oil being kept off the market by evil oil companies; *Alligator,* about those reptiles prowling the New York City sewers; and *Hangar 18,* the story of the crashed UFO and the frozen bodies found thereon being stored at Wright-Patterson Air Force Base in Ohio. Reality and fiction have been at odds on this story for a generation. One case in point was the unnamed Atlanta businessman who in 1983 offered the Air Force $3.14 for "each of the extraterrestrial alien bodies stored at

Wright-Patterson Air Force Base." *USA Today* reported on July 22, 1983, that the man wanted the bodies of "three-foot-tall, humanlike creatures wrapped in fine metallic-like cloth," which he said were found in three downed flying saucers. The Air Force told him to go away.

Scott Morris, who watches unconfirmed rumors for *Omni* magazine, sees a vast potential for related movies: "First out will be *Scallop!* about a ruthless restaurateur who serves cut-out shark or skate to unsuspecting customers who have ordered shellfish."

One saving grace for many of the credos is that they are laced with a strong tot of fun. One of the hoariest culinary stories involves the overbearing rich matron who demands that a swank hotel sell her the secret recipe for "red velvet cake." (This has happened at such hostelries as the Waldorf-Astoria in New York, the Fairmont in San Francisco, and the Roosevelt in New Orleans.) For $500 the chef finally relents. The secret: add a half cup of red food coloring to a package of regular cake mix. The Waldorf management stopped trying to deny the story decades ago (the hotel has never served red velvet cake or any approximation)—there are times when one chooses to shut up and enjoy the story along with everyone else. And, again, credos can be used to state perceptions of bitter reality. James Davis, a black correspondent and sometime collector of credos, remembers a legend told to him "by old folks when I was growing up: that if NASA ever found black folks elsewhere in the universe, this would bring space exploration to a halt."

We offer this work as a cultural way station; as an informal compilation of some of the beliefs, major and minor, that fuel our nation as we stumble toward the year 2000. Whether a credo is bogus or genuine is irrelevant: these are the things being said (and repeated) on America's streets, front pages, and airwaves. Were it possible for a sociologist or cultural anthropologist to trace each to its origin, assuredly a kernel of original truth might be found at the site.

The authors, both Mencken enthusiasts, bow with gratitude toward *The American Credo,* compiled and published by H. L. Mencken and George Jean Nathan in 1920. (These partners later split, for irrelevant reasons, and the latter carried on the credos work with two subsequent volumes issued later in the 1920s.) Our first contribution to contemporary credos was published in *The Washingtonian* magazine in July 1979. Within weeks our modest effort was heralded throughout the Republic, with the article either reprinted in or commented upon by such august journals as the *Chicago Tribune, The Dallas Morning News, The Des Moines Register, The Bulletin* of Philadelphia, and the *St. Louis Post-Dispatch.* As a means of bringing scientific order to further research, the authors created the Center for Research into Epigrammatic Dogmatic Observations (CREDO), with international headquarters at Post Office Box 80, Garrett Park, Maryland 20896. (Among the organizations that did not give·support to CREDO were the National Endowment for the Humanities, the Rockefeller Foundation, and the Page County, Virginia, Center for the Support of Creative Arts.)

In 1982 we published our first book-length version of the collection. It was titled *There Are Alligators in the Sewers and Other American Credos* and attracted considerable press attention and many letters from folks who wanted to add to the collection or express their frustration with our myth skewering. This letter from a reader whose name we have decided not to publish to protect the perplexed is typical of the latter:

June 7, 1983

Dear Sirs:

I greatly enjoyed reading your book, "There are Alligators in our Sewers."

However, if all these credos are untrue or mostly untrue, what am I to believe? You have blasted some of the very foundations of my American life and upbringing. How am I to explain to my family, friends etc. when confronted with such credos that they spout 'bunk'? How do I ascertain from now on if whatever I hear or read is true or not? What is the status of "Don't believe anything you hear and only half of what you read"?

What a philosophical dilemma for this average person.

And lastly, is it true that famous, important people (stars, politicians, *authors*) never receive or read their fan mail?

This book is the result of much new material collected over the last ten years that has been merged with material from the first book. It goes without saying that we are working a most fertile field here and the amount of new nonsense and bunk has grown in the interim.

Contributions of credos were obtained from a wide range of persons, and their kindness to the authors is more formally acknowledged at the end of the book.

CREDO intends to continue the compilation of credos, in the interest of the advancement of our contemporary culture. Persons desirous of adding their own favorite credos to the existing body of knowledge are cordially invited to communicate with the authors at the CREDO address listed above.

ANIMALS

◆ That the Smithsonian is in possession of the remains of several American animals of fantastic proportions and attributes, but that they are hidden from public view and their presence denied because they do not jibe with present-day scientific theory. For instance, the great gowrow, which was shipped to the museum in 1897 by a traveling salesman from Arkansas. It was heavily scaled, tusked, hornbacked, and twenty feet long.

◆ That giant alligators thrive in the sewer systems of our major cities as a consequence of people having bought baby alligators in Florida, then having tired of them, and finally flushed them down their toilets.

(In his book World Beneath the City, *Robert Daley reported on an interview with former New York Commissioner of Sewers Teddy May, who said that men in his department spotted two-foot-long alligators in the city's sewers in 1935. It was first assumed that the men had been drinking, but further investigation confirmed the alligators. May said that with the aid of poison and .22 rifles they were wiped out by 1937.*

This is a clear case of a belief that has a modicum of truth to it, although that truth is a far cry from the Cadillac-sized beasts of legend.)

◆ That bats are blind.

(They can see in daylight and have developed an "echo location" system for "seeing" at night.)

◆ That bats are drawn to the hair on the human head and will become tangled therein.

(Bats have more myths attached to them than almost any other creature. They do swing by the human head as they hunt for food but seldom, if ever, get into people's hair.)

◆ That bears often hug their human victims to death.

◆ That beavers can gnaw through a tree trunk and have it fall where they want it to.

(They can do no such thing, and slower members of the species have been found crushed to death by trees brought down upon them. This myth is attacked in Grame Donald's Things You Thought You Knew, *along with the notion that beavers are able to use their broad tails to pat down mud in constructing dams.)*

◆ That birds head south in the wintertime to avoid the cold.

(They migrate for food, which is far less plentiful in the North in the cold months.)

◆ That birds sing only at sunset and dawn.

◆ That bulls are infuriated by the color red.

(Although matadors wave red capes in bullfights, it is the movement that attracts the bull's attention and not the color, since bulls, like many other animals, including dogs, see only shades of light and dark.)

◆ That bumblebees are too heavy to fly but are able to fly because they are unaware of the laws of aerodynamics.

(This "fact" is often used by people who are trying to motivate others to do the impossible—"Look at the bumblebee," they say. "It can do the impossible because it does not know that it is impossible." Fact is, the bumblebee's wings move so fast that it can fly, and it, like all other things that fly, obeys the laws of aerodynamics and physics.)

◆ That if a farm boy lifts a calf every day from its birth, he will be able to lift the animal when it's fully grown.

◆ That camels store water in their humps.

◆ That cats are smarter than dogs but that dogs have better personalities.

◆ That cats reduce the mice and rat populations in a given area and that some cats are tremendous "mousers."

(A researcher at the University of Maryland, Eugene Wood, studied this question and concluded in a 1984 interview that cats tend to play with rodents and let them go, and that cat food and cat waste may actually attract mice and rats.)

◆ That any cat, given the opportunity, will hover over the crib of a baby and suck the baby's breath until it dies.

◆ That cats have the innate ability to discern supernatural presences. (Corollary: That if your cat suddenly jumps up and stares down an empty hallway, you'd best sleep with the lights on that night.)

◆ That chameleons are able to change color depending on the background they are in front of.

(Those we have encountered that do not turn plaid in front of a sport shirt are obviously either defective or some other kind of lizard. These lizards do go through slight changes in color but it has nothing to do with background; rather things such as light, temperature, or emotion.)

◆ That centipedes have 100 legs.

(Centipedes, according to the World Book Encyclopedia, *have between 28 and 340 legs.)*

◆ That cockroaches can survive in any environment, which is why they are routinely discovered in mine shafts, volcano mouths, orbiting spacecraft, and Manhattan apartments.

◆ That for every cockroach you see in your home, there are————that you don't see.

(An excerpt from a newspaper article is in order here:

That old bit of kitchen wisdom that for every roach you see, there are 10 you don't see—forget it. For every one you see there can be 1,000 you don't see, according to Richard S. Patterson, who studies cockroaches in the Agriculture Department's Insects Affecting Man and Animals Laboratory.

The recent survey was done in 550 low-income apartments in Gainesville, Florida, but Patterson added that it is not only low-income housing that has high populations of roaches. Work in the District and elsewhere shows that houses or apartments of the wealthy are also counted as potential roach havens because much food is stored and the kitchens are often run like restaurants.

—The Washington Post, *Sunday, May 18, 1986, from an article entitled "To Count Hidden Cockroaches, Multiply Visible Ones by 1,000?")*

◆ That cows lie down before a rainstorm.

(Cows, in fact, lie down when they feel like it, which is usually when they are tired.)

◆ That dinosaurs were the bane of cavemen.

(Despite the fact that the interval between the last dinosaur and the first man was at least 60 million years, this myth is still strong,

no doubt aided by countless Hollywood films in which the beasts bedevil cave dwellers.)

◆ That a dog senses the death of its master even though they are separated by many miles.

◆ That dogs are able to judge human character.

("Puzzy likes you; he knows you are honest and wouldn't be cruel to him.") Ditto for cats. ("Princess never ever sits in a stranger's lap. You must be a fine and caring person.")

◆ That you can't teach an old dog new tricks.

◆ That barking dogs don't bite.

(True, as long as they keep barking.)

◆ That you should never allow a strange dog to know that you are afraid.

◆ That dogs frequently detect fires and bark in such a way as to warn humans of the danger.

◆ That it is just a matter of time until humans and dolphins find a way to communicate. At that time the dolphin will tell us all sorts of remarkable things, including, perhaps, the full story of Atlantis.

(When this assertion is made, it is always stated in terms of what the dolphins will tell us, rather than what we'll tell them. Will we read to them from the latest issue of People *or show them the latest episode of "A Current Affair"?)*

◆ That elephants head for an immense graveyard when it is time for them to die. The location of this treasury of ivory has long eluded human discovery. Elephants recall the location of the graveyard only in their final hours.

◆ That elephants are afraid of mice.

◆ That elephants have great memories.

(They don't have bad memories, but are about average among mammals.)

◆ That foxes are so canny that they have been known to lure dogs pursuing them over railroad trestles just in time to be killed by thundering trains.

(Around the turn of the century a number of such stories were told in books by writers who never bothered to mention that these stories were fiction. This example, along with whoppers like the one about woodcocks fashioning splints out of mud for their broken wings, was

cited by Henry F. Pringle in his biography of Theodore Roosevelt as irritations to Roosevelt, who was offended by them.)

◆   That goats eat shoes and tin cans.

("Goats will lick the labels off tin cans for the salt content of the glue, and they nibble at almost anything out of curiosity, but they will not—nor can they—eat shoes or tin cans" is how Joseph Rosenbloom explained it in his 1978 book Bananas Don't Grow on Trees.*)*

◆   That a halibut has a face like a baby, and given this startling fact, the heads of all halibut are cut off at the moment they are caught.

◆   That you can lead a horse to water but you can't make him drink.

(True, if the horse has a bellyful of water, but horses usually drink when they are offered water.)

◆   That lemmings commit mass suicide by herding themselves into the ocean.

(A 1992 study by researchers at the University of British Columbia labeled this as nonsense—"a Walt Disney myth"—but did point out that the little rodents were serial killers who kill one another's offspring.

One of the researchers, Charles Krebs, told Reuter News Service in March 1992: "There's no animal that commits suicide; it's a biologically impossible concept. I will pay anybody $1,000 to show you a picture of any two or more lemmings jumping over a cliff. It does not happen.")

◆   That it does not bother or pain a lobster to be cooked alive. Nor, for that matter, does it hurt a cow when it's branded.

◆   That all the lower animals are monogamous.

◆   That mice prefer cheese to all other foods.

(Several experiments have shown that mice prefer sweets to all other foods. They will eat cheese but show no preference for it. "Those cartoons that show mice gobbling up cheese as if it were their favorite food are wrong. Mice do not prefer cheese, and often will not touch it if any other food is available," says Joseph Rosenbloom in his 1978 book Bananas Don't Grow on Trees.*)*

◆   That monkeys groom each other by looking for fleas in each other's fur.

(They do not have fleas. They are removing dead skin, which they then eat.)

◆ That somewhere in America there is a traveling carnival with an orangutan. Anyone who can last three rounds with the beast gets $500.

◆ That large octopuses can and do strangle humans.

(Only in comic strips.)

◆ That octopuses and squid release clouds of ink to hide behind.

(They do emit ink, but it is to act as a decoy, which leads an aggressor to come after the "ghost" rather than the real thing.)

◆ That ostriches hide their heads in the sand.

(What they do is bend over to pick fruit, grass, insects, and mice from the ground. That may have looked like head burying to the nearsighted observer who started this one.)

◆ That owls and cats can see in total darkness.

◆ That pigeons have a natural affinity for statues.

◆ That no one has ever seen a baby pigeon, despite years of observation of their nesting places with telephoto lenses.

◆ That porcupines are able to shoot their quills when aroused.

(A frightened porcupine runs from danger. If an enemy catches up to it, the porcupine tightens its skin to make the quills stand up, ready to lodge in anything that touches them.)

◆ That the proper way to pick up a rabbit is by its ears.

(The proper way to lift a rabbit is by the scruff of the neck.)

◆ That rats leave a sinking ship.

◆ That if you give enough of anything to a laboratory rat it will get cancer.

◆ That there are stinging snakes in the deep south that can easily kill a bull or a tree.

◆ That snakes paralyze their intended victims with a hypnotic stare.

◆ That if you hold a skunk upside down by its tail it can't spray you or anyone else.

(A story is told of a science teacher who wanted to test this theory. His former friends say that "yes, a skunk can still spray when held by its tail head down.")

◆ That whales spout water.

(Whales exhale air through blowholes, which creates a mist or fog that looks like a water spout.)

◆ That if you cut a worm in half it will grow into two worms.

(Sometimes, depending upon the type of worm. But after such a division, a worm loses much of its interest in life and dies without further ingestion or reproduction.)

◆ That they're just as afraid of us as we are of them.

(Don't bet on this one, especially when dealing with grizzly bears, sharks, and others.)

THE ARTS

◆ That all great artists are thin *(presumably because of the suffering they have had to endure).*

◆ That if it were not for *The Nutcracker* and *Swan Lake*, American ballet would have long ago ceased to exist.

◆ That while the total fraud inherent in modern abstract art is immediately obvious to the man on the street, it is totally missed by the critics, museum curators, and wealthy patrons of the arts.

◆ That the world envisioned in the paintings of Norman Rockwell was a real one, but a world that has now largely disappeared.

◆ That most furniture sold as antiques in Maine, New Hampshire, upstate New York, Massachusetts, and/or Vermont actually was made the previous winter and aged by using it in the homes of clumsy people.

◆ That some of the finest, most important, and sensitive photographs ever taken were made by amateurs with box cameras.

◆ That if the scribblings of toddlers were framed and hung on the walls of the appropriate galleries, they would sell for a small fortune and be proclaimed as the last word in abstract expressionism or minimalism.

◆   That there is a code associated with the statues of military heroes. If all four of the horse's feet are on the ground, it means that the general survived the war. If one foot is off the ground, it means that he was wounded, and two feet off the ground symbolizes death on the battlefield.

◆   That if you prowl around flea markets and garage sales long enough, you'll eventually find some unrecognized treasure at a ridiculously low price. (Corollary: That the experts come to these sales at the crack of dawn and haul away the good stuff, which is why you never find any yourself.)

(There are, of course, true stories along these lines. Two of the rarest daguerrotypes to surface in recent decades were picked up at a Freeport, Maine, flea market. The reality of it is that there are many more stories of such finds than there are true stories of such finds.)

◆   That the eyes of a portrait of a loved one or the eyes of a religious portrait, hanging on a wall, will follow you as you move in the room.

◆   That in order for a writer, poet, or artist to achieve greatness, he or she must be either neurotic or possessed of a fatal flaw . . . and live in a cold, airless garret.

◆   That people no longer know how to dance.

BUSINESS

◆   That it is un-American not to pad your expense account.

◆   That someone somewhere higher up in the organization really knows what's going on, and will be competent enough to save us when the shit hits the fan.

◆   That on a typewriter, the top row contains all the letters needed to type the word "typewriter." This was done so the machine could be easily demonstrated by salesmen.

(The first part of this is true, but the keys were arranged so that they would not jam.)

◆ That seashore building lots sold by mail solicitations are three or more feet beneath water; that "vacation-home sites" similarly marketed in the West are inaccessible patches of desert.

◆ That if an ad appears that contains an incorrectly low price, the advertiser must sell the item in question for that low price.

◆ That it pays to advertise.

◆ That renegade advertisers flash invisible-to-the-eye but subconsciously perceived messages to television viewers during commercials and programs alike.

◆ That there is a little-known federal law that prohibits retailers from announcing overly low sale prices in print advertisements or over the air. The merchant will announce his prices are "so low we can't mention them!"

◆ That nine out of ten start-up small businesses fail in their first year of operation.

◆ That White Rock's "Lady of the Lake" is still seen occasionally by teenaged couples parking on summer nights.

◆ That if the Ford Motor Company would manufacture Model A's again, they would become the biggest best-sellers in auto history; that most of what Detroit produces today are lemons.

◆ That if all American corporate presidents spent a year or so in Japan studying superior management techniques, our economy would right itself within two or three years.

◆ That American business does not get it right—but that Japanese business does.

◆ That the phone company has a secret monitoring center out in St. Louis—or maybe it's Minneapolis—where every phone conversation made in the United States is recorded on computers. These tapes are routinely given to the FBI, the CIA, and bill-collection agencies.

◆ That clicking or other noise on your phone line is a strong indication some scoundrel is tapping it.

(Unlikely, given technological advances of the past two decades.)

♦ That it is possible to devise better things for better living through chemistry.

♦ That the name of the retail chain of E. J. Korvette was short for "Eight Jewish Korean War Veterans."

(Korvette founder Eugene Ferkauf explained in his book Going into Business *that the E was for his first name, the J was for that of associate and pal Joe Swillenberg, and the* Korvette *was picked because it has a "euphonious ring." He got it from the name of the Canadian war vessel corvette and changed the C to a K when he found it illegal to register the name of a naval-class identity.)*

♦ That copulating polar bears and the like are drawn into the photographs of drinks in liquor ads to help sell the product. Although hard to find with the naked eye, these sexual images work on us subliminally.

♦ That you should buy razor blades during the World Series (or during other times when the companies that make them sponsor advertising blitzes), as they are purposely made sharper then, so that anyone trying them for the first time will be so amazed and impressed that he will become a lifetime customer.

♦ That the bottom blade in a razor blade package is the sharpest.

♦ That any car salesman worth his salt will come back from his manager's office, after taking him *your* best offer for that car you want, with his tail dragging between his legs, saying, "Whew! He really chewed my ——— out on this one! I tried like crazy to get that price for you. But the best I can do is . . ."

♦ That owners of small businesses spend all of their time filling out forms devised by federal bureaucrats.

♦ That no shortages are real: somewhere off both coasts are ships holding great quantities of crude oil, sirloin steak, and cotton bales, to drive up the prices.

♦ That electric utilities periodically overload their lines to burn out light bulbs. Some go out at once, others survive for a few hours. But if one light bulb burns out, two or three others will follow within a day. The manufacturers of bulbs pay the utilities to perform this service, because under normal circumstances the bulbs would last for years.

Also, that the same parties have long conspired to prevent the appearance of a truly long-lasting "lifetime" electric light bulb—something that has been technically possible for decades.

(Without resorting to editorial comment, we quote herewith from a report, "The Short Life of the Electric Light Bulb," issued in October 1966 by the Government Activities Subcommittee of the House Committee on Government Operations, commencing at page one:

Over the 87 years since Edison perfected the bulb, there have been countless improvements in bulb design and product efficiency.

Yet not one improvement ever made has been toward increasing bulb life. The standard 100-watt bulb—the most popular size in American homes—was designed to burn 800 hours in 1908. This was increased to 1,000 hours in 1910. But, on April 1, 1933, the bulb industry made sweeping reductions in the life of all standard household variety bulbs. The 100-watt bulb was reduced from 1,000 to 750 hours, where it remains today.... There is scarcely an individual who has not harbored the suspicion that bulb manufacturers intentionally design bulbs to burn out quickly so that they may sell more bulbs at the consumers' expense.

(The committee quoted the manufacturers' response that bulbs designed to last longer would consume more power, thereby offsetting any economic advantage for the consumer.)

◆   That with hard work you can achieve anything you want to in the United States.

◆   That if one writes a letter of complaint about certain products, the response will be to get a case of that product in compensation.

◆   That all gasoline is the same, and tanker trucks from a number of companies routinely line up to be supplied from a common source.

◆   That every Tuesday or so a malcontent assembly-line worker puts a handful of gravel into the hubcap of a new Cadillac, along with a note intended to be found weeks later that reads, "So you finally found the rattle, you rich SOB!"

◆   That people who live in towns with horrible industrial odors not only learn to live with the smell but invariably tell outsiders who mention it, "That's the smell of money."

♦ That any crowd at an auction contains at least three shills whose duty is to bid up prices for the item you really want. They stand in separate parts of the room and do not acknowledge that they know one another or the auctioneer.

♦ That if it weren't for the excesses of big labor, big business, and big government, there would be no inflation.

♦ That a Rolls-Royce engine is sealed when the car leaves the factory and must not be touched by any mechanic save an expert dispatched from Great Britain. If a Rolls-Royce breaks down anytime during its life warranty, the manufacturer will fly a mechanic to the owner's location, wherever it may be, to make the repairs.

♦ That foreign [fill in the blank: automakers, steelmakers, etc.] are unfair.

FALLING HEMLINES AND OTHER MARKET BAROMETERS

• That falling hemlines on women's fashions are a forewarning of financial panics; that shorter skirts mean go-go soars in the Dow Jones industrial average.

• That if a team that is in the National Football Conference, or was in the original NFL, wins the Super Bowl, the stock market will rise during the year. The NFL and the old American Football Conference played four inter-league championship matches (1967–1970) before merging.

This uncannily accurate harbinger was first noted by Robert Stovall when he was with the old Dean Witter Reynolds brokerage firm, who found that it held true for fifteen of the first sixteen Super Bowls. [The one exception was 1970, when the AFC's Kansas City Chiefs beat the NFC's Minnesota Vikings. The Standard & Poor 500 nonetheless was up slightly at year's end.] Here is a year-by-year tabulation of the Super Bowl winners and the Dow Jones industrial average at the close of the year. NFC/original NFL teams are in boldface and italics.

1967	*Green Bay Packers* 35,	Kansas City Chiefs 10	905.11
1968	*Green Bay Packers* 33,	Oakland Raiders 14	943.75
1969	New York Jets 16,	*Baltimore Colts* 7	800.36
1970	Kansas City Chiefs 23,	*Minnesota Vikings* 7	838.92
1971	*Baltimore Colts* 16,	Dallas Cowboys 13	890.20
1972	*Dallas Cowboys* 24,	Miami Dolphins 3	1020.20
1973	Miami Dolphins 14,	*Washington Redskins* 7	850.86
1974	Miami Dolphins 24,	*Minnesota Vikings* 7	616.24
1975	Pittsburgh Steelers 16,	*Minnesota Vikings* 6	825.41
1976	*Pittsburgh Steelers*, 21	Dallas Cowboys 17	1004.65
1977	Oakland Raiders 32,	*Minnesota Vikings* 14	835.15
1978	*Dallas Cowboys* 27,	Denver Broncos 10	934.37
1979	*Pittsburgh Steelers* 35,	Dallas Cowboys 31	838.74
1980	*Pittsburgh Steelers* 31,	Los Angeles Rams 19	963.99
1981	Oakland Raiders 27,	*Philadelphia Eagles* 10	875.00
1982	*San Francisco 49ers* 26,	Cincinnati Bengals 21	1,046.54
1983	*Washington Redskins* 27,	Miami Dolphins 17	1,258.64
1984	Los Angeles Raiders 38,	*Washington Redskins* 9	1,211.57
1985	*San Francisco 49ers* 38,	Miami Dolphins 16	1,546.67
1986	*Chicago Bears* 46,	New England Patriots 10	1,895.95
1987	*New York Giants* 39,	Denver Broncos 20	1,938.83
1988	*Washington Redskins* 42,	Denver Broncos 10	2,168.57
1989	*San Francisco 49ers* 20,	Cincinnati Bengals 16	2,753.20
1990	*San Francisco 49ers* 55,	Denver Broncos 10	2,653.20
1991	*New York Giants* 20,	Buffalo Bills 19	3,168.83
1992	*Washington Redskins* 37,	Buffalo Bills 24	3,301.11

Wall Street reporter Arthur Howe described a medley of stock market theories for *American Way Magazine* in April 1984, ranging from planetary alignments to sunspots (if the number exceeds fifty per month, the market declines) and hemlines (the higher the skirt, the higher the market). Howe notes that the hemline theory started in the 1920s, the generation of short-skirted flappers and soaring stock prices. Here are other indicators from the Howe collection:

• *Snuff.* An increase in snuff sales precedes a rise in the market. Unskilled workers buy the most snuff, and they are the first to be hired when a recovery gets under way. When business drops, they are the first workers furloughed.

• *Cardboard boxes.* When manufacturers buy increased amounts of shipping cartons, more goods will be moving into stores, and presumably sold.

• *Beer cans.* Keep an eye on the side of the road. Folks buy more beer during good times and toss empties out the window. *(Under this theory, parts of the rural south and west should be in a perpetual boom.)*

• *Dog food.* A harbinger of bad times, because the truly poor turn to pet food when they can't afford other groceries.

• *Peanut butter.* Austin Kiplinger, the Washington newsletter guru, says peanut butter sales are a good indicator of which way the economy is going. As he told the columnist Betty Beale of the old Washington *Star* on August 1, 1988, "When consumers think the economy's headed for a slump or they're worried about their jobs, they stock up on peanut butter. It's nourishing and a lot cheaper than meat. When things are looking good, they buy more of other foods and less p.b."

"The Boston Snow Index," developed by Drexel Burnham Lambert Inc. in 1978, holds that when there is snow on the ground in Boston on Christmas Day, stocks move up the following year.

Vartanig G. Vartan reported on this theory in *The New York Times* on November 22, 1982, and gave some mixed results: "A white Christmas in Boston preceded a higher stock market in seven of ten years. No snow on the ground was followed by an up market in 10 of 17 years."

Vartan also reported on "The Presidential Signal"—that since the Coolidge Administration, stocks have declined in the first year of every term when a Republican occupied the White House.

THE DIRTY-BUSINESS RUMOR
WARNING! DANGER ZONE! WARNING!

The following credos and rumors are **ABSOLUTELY UN-TRUE** and have already caused great damage to those involved. Use only as examples of how **WRONGHEADED** rumors can get.

Anyone quoting them as true and referring to the fact that they read them in this book will be subject to the following

CURSE: FOR ALL ETERNITY YOUR READING WILL BE RESTRICTED TO NATIONAL

TABLOIDS FOUND IN SUPERMARKET CHECKOUT LANES.

THE MANAGEMENT

During the 1970s Dr. Frederick Koenig, a social psychologist then at Tulane University in New Orleans, did a study of harmful rumors circulated about consumer products—everything from the fried rat found in a carryout family bucket of chicken to the mouse in the pop bottle. Koenig at first suspected that these lies might have been spawned by companies wishing to damage a competitor. But he eventually concluded that the vast majority are spread by "your average, person-next-door rumormonger," as he told John M. McGuire of the *St. Louis Post-Dispatch* in an article published October 16, 1978. A planted rumor runs the risk of backfiring, with the wrong company ending up the brunt of the rumor.

Koenig first encountered the dirty-business rumor as a lad in St. Louis during the 1930s, when he went into a drugstore to buy a package of cigarettes. The clerk sold them to him, but passed along a warning: he had "heard" from someone or another that the cigarette company had an employee with leprosy working in one of its factories. Anyone who smoked the cigarettes risked becoming afflicted with leprosy. A more detailed version Koenig heard later had the cigarette company buying its tobacco from a leper colony. Jerry O'Leary, who encountered the story while working for the old Washington *Star,* said his version had a leper losing a finger in the cigarette company's packaging plant.

Years later, as an academic researcher, Koenig noted that the brand of cigarettes was no longer marketed. It had paid the ultimate price of a rumor: extinction. Indeed, the manufacturer had even expunged the brand from its corporate memory; Koenig noted that executives said they had never even heard of it.

Here is a sampling of some of the false stories that have plagued American companies through the years:

♦ That Dr Pepper is made from prune juice.

♦ That Pepperidge Farm pretzels contain lye.

♦ That a woman once found a dead mouse in a bottle of Coca-Cola, sued for a million dollars, and won.

♦ That several months before Gillette puts a new razor blade on the market it deliberately lowers the quality of the current line. A man who has been comfortable shaving with a Gillette platinum finds that it drags and cuts. So he buys the Gillette Sensor Super and is happy. In fact, the Sensor is no better than the Sensor marketed during the 1940s.

♦ That spider eggs have been found in Bubble Yum; McDonald's hamburgers have been beefed up with ground worms; and Pop Rocks have exploded in kids' stomachs.

♦ That Teflon-contaminated cigarettes have killed; welders have been blown into tiny pieces because they carried butane lighters in their pockets; and the secret of a popular cigarette filter is that it uses ground glass.

♦ That when a person turns fifty-seven, he can write to the Heinz food company and get a free carton of Heinz products.

(Actually this was true until the 1950s, according to Rudy Maxa in his Washington Post *column for March 21, 1982.)*

♦ That Girl Scout cookies, along with other popular products, are laced with THC or hashish, and that consumers routinely discover Kentucky-fried rats, charbroiled fingers, and worse in fast-food restaurants.

There have been more in the same vein: a long-running rumor that a Church's Fried Chicken was the agent of black sterilization and an insane story about white doctors giving AIDS to black patients on purpose or that, more simply, AIDS was a form of genocide aimed at African-Americans.

(This may have been assisted by a KGB disinformation campaign

of the early '80s saying that deadly virus was a product of a Pentagon experiment gone haywire.)

Collectively, these untruisms have cost the companies involved a quadruple king's ransom running campaigns to dispel them. Squibb, which owns Bubble Yum, spent more than $100,000 trying to kill the spider-egg falsehood, and Pepperidge Farm was compelled to put one of its top executives on the television talk-show circuit to spike the lye lie by eating pretzels in front of the camera.

THE DEVIL IN THE LOGO

But for some corporations, farfetched rumors have proved far more than a nuisance. Beginning in the 1970s religious nuts spread the lie that devil worshipers had taken control of Procter & Gamble, as evidenced by the man-in-the-moon symbol in its corporate logo. Procter & Gamble patiently noted that the logo had been used, in varying forms, since 1850. The symbol began with a crude cross, which a wharf hand had painted on a wooden box of P&G "star candles." Illiterate workers used such symbols as a shipping "sign language" to tell what was in otherwise unmarked crates. Too, customers asked for "the candles with the star on the box." In time the cross evolved into a star within a circle, and then into a circle containing thirteen stars representing the original thirteen colonies of the United States. The "man in the moon" joined the stars in the circle in 1882, the year the symbol was registered with the U.S. Patent Office. It had no secret satanic meaning. The man in the moon is facing thirteen stars that represent the original thirteen colonies of the United States.

What especially irked P&G is that its products have "always been marketed on themes of purity and wholesomeness," as Baltimore public relations consultant William Amelia noted in a *New York Times* Op Ed piece on August 14, 1982. Indeed, Harley Procter, a son of one of the founders, resorted to a passage in the Book of Psalms for the name of one of its most popular products, Ivory Soap: "All thy garments smell of myrrh, and aloes, and cassia, out of ivory palaces, whereby they have made thee glad." So what is a company to do when a seventy-five-year-old woman writes: "In the beginning, God made the tree. Where did Satan get Charmin?" Other (false) reports reaching the company claimed that a P&G executive had boosted satanism on a national television talk show and said that some of the firm's profits went to the Church of Satan.

In the summer of 1982 the corporation sued more than half a dozen persons it accused of perpetuating the myth. At one time P&G was receiving an incredible 12,000 written queries monthly about the canard. Nonetheless, fundamentalist preachers and peddlers of rival sundries persisted in spreading the "Satan runs P&G" rumor.

P&G circulated statements from producers of such popular TV shows as "Donahue" and "60 Minutes" attesting that no P&G executive had endorsed satanism on their programs. Religious figures such as the Reverend Don Wildmon denounced the rumors in their publications.

Nonetheless, the satan stories persisted, and in 1985 P&G gave up the struggle and dropped the man-in-the-moon symbol from its logo. A company spokesman told the Associated Press in an article published in many papers on April 25, 1985: "The bottom line is that the move is being made because there appears to be little advantage to having the trademark on product packages. At the same time, it will remove one part of those false and malicious stories." But P&G did retain the symbol on its corporate stationery and buildings.

The satan rumor also bedeviled McDonald's Corporation during the 1970s, with Bible Belt fanatics boycotting the hamburger chain because of the notion that founder Ray Kroc gave vast sums to the Church of Satan. The story was absolutely false. Kroc joined the Harnard Congregational Church in Oak Park, Illinois, at age seven and attended services there for more than seventy years, until his death.

Nonetheless, the rumor was spread by persons who claimed to have heard Kroc vow allegiance to the devil during an interview on the Phil Donahue television show in mid-1977. He had appeared to promote a book about his life as a hamburger tycoon. McDonald's widely distributed tapes of the show demonstrating that Kroc made no such statements.

Confronted with this evidence, the rumormongers replied, "Well, tapes can be erased; remember Richard Nixon and Watergate?"

The afore-cited Professor Koenig of Tulane said the McDonald's lie was a classic example of "the rumor used as an act of aggression." He said, "People like to start rumors about big companies, the so-called 'king' industries, and big government. It gives a sense of importance for people who need a sense of importance. People who are fairly secure about their positions and their lives do not spread rumors."

McDonald's eventually put the rumor to rest by threatening drastic legal action against people who spread it by leaflets and word of mouth. "Apparently the golden arches do not resemble the gates of hell," columnist Cal Thomas wrote on May 2, 1985, in *The Washington Times.*

Not surprisingly, religious fanatics require scant evidence when they level charges of satanism. *The Reporter,* a daily newspaper published in Martinsville, Indiana, reproduces in its masthead the famed "Don't tread on me" flag of the American Revolution. Anonymous letters accused the paper of supporting devil worship through the flag. Robert Kendall, feisty publisher of the Martinsville *Daily Record,* who detests nonsense of all sorts, refused to pay heed to "a wave of hysteria generated by people with more imagination than sense." He wrote on August 14, 1991: "I believe we'll keep our snake, unless they can give us probative evidence that the Founding Father who designed it was a warlock instead of a warrior."

THE KKK AND SODA POP

A business besieged with a false rumor faces a Hobson's choice. An unchallenged lie spreads. ("If it isn't true, why aren't they denying it?") But the very act of denial publicizes the report. Arlene Levinson of the Associated Press told of a New York bottling company's response to a rumor campaign in the summer of 1991. (Ms. Levinson's story ran in various papers on August 1, 1991.) Brooklyn Bottling Company was struggling on the brink of bankruptcy, relying on sales of seltzer water. Eric Miller inherited the company in the mid-1980s and re-

vived an old line of fruit-flavored sodas and renamed them
"Tropical Fantasy." Aiming at a long-income market, he had a
suggested retail price of 49¢ for a 20-ounce container, far below that charged by competitive brands. Sales skyrocketed.
Then, disaster. Handbills were circulated in Harlem carrying
an absolutely false statement about Tropical Fantasy and drinks
made by another company:

ATTENTION!! ATTENTION!! ATTENTION!!!
**Please be advised, Top Pop, and Tropical Fantasy, also 50 sodas
are being manufactured by the Ku Klux Klan.**
**Sodas contain stimulants to sterilize the black man, and who
knows what else!!!**
You have been warned. Please save the children.

The rumor quickly spread all over New York, and then to
adjoining states. Kids found distributing the false fliers said that
"some guy" had given them $5. But what guy? No one knew.
When a Miller driver went into a Coney Island neighborhood
people stoned his truck, yelling, "Get out of here! You sterilize
blacks!" Cases of unsold sodas stacked up in stores.

Miller thought the campaign of lies particularly outrageous
because most of his 125 workers were minorities, and he was
giving poorer consumers a good deal on soda. So he hired a
public relations firm and told the media of the lie. Major
newspapers and the minority press ran editorials that warned
against believing harmful nonsense.

The anti-rumor climax came when Mayor David Dinkins,
who is African-American, agreed to drink Tropical Fantasy on
television. Within a month Brooklyn Bottling's business was
back to normal. The Kings County District Attorney's Office
and a detective agency tried to find who was responsible for
the rumor, but with no success.

Lorraine Hale, a psychologist and president of Hale House
Foundation, tried to explain why such lies are believed. She
told Ms. Levinson of the Associated Press, "Having come from
a slavery background, where we were so brutalized for so long,
the sense of fear we have as a people is very real. There's a mass

paranoia that the objective here is to kill us out, as easily and quickly as possible. We don't articulate it, but we act upon it."

CHILDREN

◆ That children suffer from growing pains.
◆ That making a child walk too early will give him bowed legs.
◆ That children should always wear clean underwear just in case they are involved in an accident and have to be undressed in the hospital.
◆ That children who attend Catholic parochial school are more given to swearing and telling dirty jokes than public-school kids.
◆ That prodigies start off with a bang but soon peter out.
◆ That most boys who grow up to amount to something have had newspaper routes and belonged to the Boy Scouts.
◆ That the proper college fraternity gives a young man an immeasurable boost up the ladder of success.
◆ That military service exerts a calming influence on young men.
◆ That a child born in the summer will tend to be smarter than one born during any other season.
(This belief has been so widespread that studies were conducted to see if it had any validity. The answer, as reported in the British Medical Journal *for March 4, 1944, is that it is untrue.)*
◆ That children of right-wing parents grow up to flame as liberals, and vice versa.
◆ That children with high IQs tend to be sicklier and not as well adjusted as those with normal or low IQs. The lower-IQ kids will grow up to be more successful in their jobs and marriages.
(All of this is absolutely false, according to Lewis Terman, a Stanford psychologist who has studied children with higher IQs.)

◆ That children always grow taller than their parents.

◆ That the youngest child is always spoiled and, consequently, worthless.

◆ That daughters tend to resemble their mothers, after sufficient time.

◆ That the oldest child is the leader or most mature emotionally.

◆ That a quiet child is a good child.

◆ That if you awaken a sleepwalking child, he might die from fright.

◆ That children of large families are more "normal" or well adjusted than children of small families.

◆ That any boy or girl can grow up to be president of the United States.

◆ That daughters like their dads best, and vice versa.

◆ That if a nine-year-old boy digs a hole through the earth from any location in the United States, he will emerge in China.

◆ That the offspring of first cousins are likely to be feeble-minded.

◆ That powerful families go to hell in the third generation of power.

◆ That older parents give birth to smarter but physically weaker children.

◆ That, according to your child, things that have dubious value have hidden value. That video games improve one's eye-hand coordination and that watching Saturday cartoons allows one to keep one's clothes clean.

SMALL BOY CREDOS

• That the only suitable way to break in a new catcher's mitt is to fit a baseball into the desired "pocket" and bind the mitt tightly with leather thongs for several days. The resultant pocket will be permanent and enable the small boy to perform on a par with Cal Ripkin or Jose Canseco.

• That no pocketknife with less than seven blades is worth carrying around.

• That if you step on a grave in a cemetery, the deceased won't be comfortable until he has retaliated by coming around to haunt you some night.
• That if you have a dream about falling and actually "hit" before awakening you will die.
• That if you walk down Michigan Avenue in Chicago there is a good chance that you will run into Michael Jordan and other members of the Chicago Bulls basketball team.

CITIES AND STATES

◆ That as Maine goes, so goes the nation.
◆ That New York, Washington, and Los Angeles are so far from the norm that people from those places cannot possibly know what the rest of the country is thinking.
◆ That all New Yorkers are loud, New Englanders stoic, southerners slow, and Californians fast.
◆ That New Yorkers can live in a place for many years and never get to know their neighbors.
◆ That New York might be fun to visit, but no sensible person would live there.
◆ That civilization does not exist west of the Hudson River nor south of the Battery.
◆ That people in Los Angeles couldn't care less about either viewpoint—to them civilization is centered on the freeway.
◆ That people in New York City are offered so many cultural events that they find it hard to decide which to attend and therefore end up going to fewer plays, concerts, et cetera, than the average person from Milwaukee.
◆ That native Washingtonians are exceedingly hard to find in the District of Columbia, and that in the District you are

much more likely to find someone born in Atlanta or Los Angeles.

◆ That there is no J Street in Northwest Washington, D.C.— between I and K Streets—because Pierre L'Enfant, who designed the city, was feuding with Chief Justice John Jay.

(An article by Jonathan Croner in The Washington Post *stated: ". . . this story has not been proved false; but there appears to be no solid evidence supporting it and there probably never will be.")*

◆ That children in Baltimore learn by their sixth birthday not to inhale through their noses because of: (a) the Exxon refinery in East Baltimore, (b) the mounds of rotting crab shells behind each house, and (c) the inner harbor. This odd way of breathing explains their accent.

◆ That residents of Pittsburgh have to remind themselves not to order boilermakers when they are out of town; that they are distinguished for callused hands and incomprehensible accents.

◆ That Chicago is excessively windy and that anyone coming back from the "Windy City" should complain about how bad it was.

(Joseph Rosenbloom points out in his Bananas Don't Grow on Trees *that Chicago, according to the U.S. Weather Bureau, ranks sixteenth on the list of the nation's windiest cities after such places as Boston and Dallas. Writing in the* Chicago Tribune *April 12, 1983, columnist Bill Granger reported on the origin of the term. "This moniker came from Charles Dana, a newspaper editor in New York who wrote fiery editorials against Chicago when we tried to take the World's Fair away from New York in 1892. Dana said Chicago was a 'windy city' because of all the hot air from all the politicians and businessmen trying to sell this town to the world.")*

◆ That everything is up to date in Kansas City.

◆ That to Iowans the smell of manure is the smell of money.

◆ That Boston has a logical plan and that it is possible to ride around the city without a map.

◆ That if tipped properly, any waitress in Nashville, Tennessee, will pick up her guitar and sing you a C&W song on the spot.

◆ That most of the people in New Orleans are decadents who carry on in the rich tradition of onetime resident Tennessee Williams, although some of the older folks are now slowing down and go to bed at four A.M. rather than dawn.

♦   That you still had best not speak evil of Huey Long in the rural backwoods of Louisiana, although you can risk a joke about Uncle Earl once the people get to know you.

♦   That a true Texan wears cowboy boots, a western hat, and chews Red Man.

♦   That the "real rich" oilmen in Dallas and Houston disdain Neiman-Marcus clothes and dress in the khakis and work boots they came to like while roughnecking in East Texas and the Permian Basin; their hobbies are collecting college football teams and Texas senators.

♦   That most of the people in Salt Lake City are Mormons, and federal law notwithstanding, polygamy persists, albeit oh so quietly.

♦   That Las Vegas can be a cheap vacation if you don't gamble—they practically give the food away.

♦   That if you stand at the corner of Hollywood and Vine there is a good chance you will spot some of the top movie stars.

(There is a better chance that you will be accosted by drug dealers and prostitutes.)

♦   That Los Angeles is without a downtown and therefore is "six suburbs in search of a city."

♦   That children in southern California are given a surfboard for their sixth birthday and admonished that they are now on their own.

♦   That the residents of Marin County, California, spend their weekends in hot tubs, sipping white wine and sighing.

♦   That the prettiest women in America are to be seen on the streets of Washington, Dallas, Houston, Los Angeles, Chicago, Philadelphia, Boston, or any one of 3,187 other cities and towns, depending on where the male watcher met his wife.

♦   That certain cities and towns are "Depression-proof" because of the basic nature of the goods or services that they provide (such as fuse boxes, oatmeal, and buttons).

(This claim is made by Chamber of Commerce people who forget that few, if any, places were spared by the economic ravages of the Great Depression.)

♦   That it is impossible to start a business, or even to get a job, in Salt Lake City unless you join the Mormon Church.

NEW YORK CREDOS OF 1930

Writing in a credo section of Thayer Hobson's *Morrow's Alma-nack and Every-Day-Book for 1930,* Burton Rascoe insisted that there was a "credo of the average New Yorker as distinct from the credo of residents of other cities." A small sampling from Rascoe's original set of thirty-nine:

• That Philadelphia is so dull and slow a town that the average citizen there doesn't know the Civil War is over.

• That the residents of Boston live exclusively on beans and codfish and that even streetcar conductors and coal bearers there use five-syllable words and talk like a page out of Emerson's essays.

• That Kalamazoo, Michigan, which is a great manufacturing city, must, because of its name, be a jerkwater town.

• That the patrons of New York nightclubs are exclusively out-of-town buyers who are painting the town red on company expense accounts.

• That mosquitoes grow as big as jaybirds in New Jersey.

• That all the residents of Brooklyn pronounce "early" as "oily" and "oily" as "early"; that they say "boids" for "birds" and "berl" for "boil."

• That there are deaths every week from falling elevators in department stores, but that the matter is hushed up by the newspapers for fear that the stores will withdraw their advertising.

• That before a girl can get a job in the chorus of a musical show she has to yield her virtue to the producer.

• That you can get a finer meal at the Automat than you can at the Ritz (the Automat closed in 1990).

• That telephone operators at the switchboards of the big hotels invariably listen in on the conversation of the guests.

THE COLLEGE PROFESSOR'S CREDOS

A college professor, Dallas Brozik, was asked for some credos from his vast storehouse of "received wisdom." In a watershed letter to the authors of this book dated February 16, 1993, he offered some of his best to us. The most interesting section of that letter was a sampling of current campus "wisdom," which we offer here:

The only three things more boring than an accountant are garden slugs and two forms of tree moss. (This is not a credo! There is supporting research.)

From the point of view of the male college student, girls from town are more promiscuous than coeds.

From the point of view of community males, college coeds are more promiscuous than girls from town.

(Having been in both camps, I would like to be able to attest to the truth of either. Unfortunately, I grew up in the Midwest during an era when the word "promiscuous" was not learned until after you had been married for several years and happened to run across the term in the description of a certain Congressperson's extralegislative activities.)

On any given university campus, there are four basic groupings of faculty members: liberal/fine arts, education, science, and business. Any three groups hold the following opinion of the fourth group, and all would be willing to defend their perceptions to any blue-ribbon panel examining the structure of the university salaries:

Liberal/Fine Arts: This is a group of fluffy-headed clowns who cannot find their backsides with both hands. If it were not for their sinecure within the educational system, they would be driving a cab, and getting lost.

Education: This is a group of fluffy-headed clowns who do not recognize that education deals with the learning of facts and skills that can be useful rather than the learning of interpersonal techniques that result in students who are comfortable with each other, until it comes time to select who actually gets a job. If it were not for their sinecure within the educational system, they would be driving a cab, and losing tips because they annoyed their fares with idle chatter.

Science: This is a group of fluffy-headed clowns who cannot stay focused long enough to hold down jobs in industry. If it were not for their sinecure within the educational system, they would be driving a cab, and getting lost because they get distracted by the theory of colors in traffic lights and whether or not there is a shorter way between points A and B.

Business: This is a group of fluffy-headed clowns who think they are too smart to work in industry. If it were not for their sinecure within the educational system, they would be driving a cab, and getting arrested for trying to sucker their fares into a Ponzi scheme.

THE CREDO-
MONGER—
A GERMANE
DIGRESSION

This might seem to be a good time to take a moment out and ask where all these wrongheaded notions and myths come from. Are any of them, in fact, plants—hoaxes, willing deviations from the truth?

There are a number of sources that create and feed them. Consider the impact of what is revealed in this clipping sent to us by a reader of the Lewiston (ME) *Daily Sun* of January 19, 1986:

MIRACLE CAR WAS
TOO GOOD TO BE TRUE

PORTLAND, OREGON—Commercials on several local radio stations described the Stardrive 2000 as a car of the future that needed no gasoline, required service every 200,000 miles and could accelerate from zero to 50 mph in 5.2 seconds.

The price was less than $8,000 and the car was to be available February 1 "at a dealer near you."

Sound too good to be true? It was.

The Stardrive 2000 was unmasked Friday as an advertising experiment conceived and sponsored by the Portland Area Radio Council, which hoped it would show how effective radio is as an advertising tool.

Friday, after a crush of press inquiries and pressure from the Oregon attorney general's office, the council began broadcasting spots acknowledging that the car did not exist. The ads unveiling the hoax had not been scheduled to air until next week.

"We are in the middle of looking at the situation," said Jan Margosian, consumer information coordinator in the financial fraud division of the attorney general's office.

She said the advertising campaign for a nonexistent product appeared to violate various provisions of the Unlawful Trade Practices Act, which permits fines of up to $25,000 per violation.

Think of all the people who now believe that the Stardrive 2000 has been kept off the market by General Motors and its coconspirators in Detroit and Japan.

There are others—a small handful of born hoaxers—who gleefully and willingly add to the confusion. Consider for a moment this letter, which came to the authors from a correspondent whom we have decided to allow to remain anonymous. The letter, which was dated December 31, 1992, amounts to a confession by a major manufacturer and distributor of this stuff.

Good to hear from you again and to learn that you're revamping ALLIGATORS ... perhaps I can contribute a few Credos to the effort. As you may know, I was inspired by Mencken's Bathtub Hoax to do a series of hoaxes myself a couple of years ago, all of which can be stated as Credos. I sent you the first, "National Cathedral Haunted?", a couple of years ago—some of the others are amongst the enclosed material, checked in red. The Hell story is a real classic and I've just sent out my hoax based on it—will send you a copy when it sees print. Here's the Credos extracted from my hoaxes:

◆ That the National Cathedral is riddled with sacrilegious images and may be haunted.

◆ That the Men in Black (MIB) associated with UFO sightings are also linked to the powerful Trilateral Commission which some people think secretly runs the world.

◆ That military equipment returning from the Gulf War inadvertently brought a vicious insect, the jumping scorpion, into this country from Iraq.

◆ That Sunday Schools are deliberately made boring and stupid to discourage interest in religion and undermine Christianity.

◆ That the Men in Black are linked to the Kennedy assassination, Watergate and numerous other scandals and conspiracies.

◆ That cows that listen to Elvis songs produce more milk and less methane.

◆ That the phrase "New World Order" was coined by Bush/Quayle to capitalize on the 500th anniversary of Columbus' "discovery" of the New World.

◆ That changing to and from Daylight Savings time causes confusion which results in many accidents and deaths each year.

◆ That extreme heat, poverty and overcrowding sometimes causes swarming behavior in humans, similar to the swarming of bees.

◆ That the JFK assassination was actually Kennedy's plan to commit suicide.

◆ That the Men in Black are linked to the POWs and MIAs from recent wars.

◆ That scientists have discovered that Hell is only 9 miles down, causing a major theological debate in the religious community.

That's enough to get started.

Peace.

What inspired this soul to this work? One major factor that has given him strength was an item from *The Oakland Tribune* entitled "Discovery of Hell a Red-Hot Rumor," which had been distributed by the Religion News Service. To quote from that article:

You think you've heard them all? How about the one about a group of geologists who drilled a hole nine miles deep in Siberia and accidentally discovered hell, complete with screams of the damned?

The Siberia story is only the latest in a series of seemingly intractable rumors that persist in some segments of the religious community despite preposterous claims and/or a complete lack of documentation.

The tale from the frozen tundra of Siberia, though, may be the hottest of them all.

Thus far, it has been repeated, with varying degrees of skepticism, in the pages of Christianity Today, the Biblical Archeology Review, and the All Africa Press Service, which is linked to the All Africa Conference of Churches.

The story goes like this:

According to a report in a Finnish newspaper, scientists from a joint European drilling project drilled nine miles into the earth, where they recorded a temperature of over 2,000 degrees Fahrenheit.

Hoping to listen to the earth's movements, they lowered microphones into the hole.

What the scientists heard was not geological rumblings but the screams of humans—at least thousands, perhaps millions—in pain. They had apparently hit hell.

Out of fear, at least half of the scientists quit. Finnish and Norwegian scientists were offered huge bribes to keep quiet about the discovery.

Fearing for their lives, they took the bribes but spoke out upon their return home.

The story has circulated for at least a year—the Christianity Today article ran in July 1990—and it is still being repeated.

The All Africa Press Service ran a story in its July 29 issue, quoting from the Biblical Archeology Review article of November/December 1990. But, showing some journalistic skepticism, the press service checked the story out with a Finnish embassy official, who said he felt it was not true.

Biblical Archeology Review, saying the story had been passed along by a reader in Starkville, Miss., printed it without a disclaimer. But the magazine prefaced its account with reference to two other purported "discoveries"—of Noah's Ark and the Ark of the Covenant, both previously debunked in the pages of the review.

When a number of readers complained about the story, Biblical Archeology Review responded with a note headlined, "Honest, We Were Only Kidding!"

The note said, "We thought the claim that hell was discovered ... was so inherently ridiculous that our readers would get a laugh over the story, just as we did."

The letter from our credomongering friend also came with a number of items and articles from small newsletters and magazines in which this man publishes his material—that is, where his mythical inventions are offered to the gullible.

Here is one of those clippings:

JUMPING SCORPIONS COME ON DOWN!

Leapin' lizards, first it was the Fire Ants, then it was the Killer Bees, now it's the Jumping Scorpions—the latest critters to be invading our once sacred shores. This time the unwanted aliens are sneaking into the US on military equipment coming back from the Middle East after America's triumphant victory over Saddam Hussein. Stowing away on the undersides of jeeps, trucks and tanks, the arachnids of Iraq have already been found in the deserts of the American southwest, mainly in Texas but also in California, Utah, Arizona and New Mexico.

The unusual scorpion, also called the butcher scorpion and even "the mother of all scorpions," goes by the scientific moniker of *Smezovis boreus,* and is characterized by its unusual legs which are much larger than other scorpions and which give it the power to jump up to four feet or more, something no other scorpion is known to do. Scientists speculate that the unique ability to jump evolved in this particular class of scorpions because of the shifting sands in southern Iraq and northern Saudi Arabia, sands which would likely cover any animal that didn't have the ability to jump out of harm's way.

The jumping scorpion is small by scorpion standards, which may be one reason that they've managed to enter this country undetected. Ranging from one to three inches and wearing an angry black-and-white striped pattern, the scorpions are probably no more dangerous than any others of their kind, but their sting is still very painful and potentially fatal to those who are allergic to them. The crablike pinchers on the front legs are sharper and more powerful than the conventional scorpion and are reported to be able to cut and slice up their victims, an ability giving rise to the label of "butcher."

Pentagon officials report that everything possible was done to make sure that no contamination of the American environment would take place as a result of the War in the Gulf. All equipment was thoroughly cleaned and inspected before it was returned to the United States, sources said, but of course no one can guarantee that something so small and undetectable as the jumping scorpion would not slip through simply because it *is* so small and undetectable. Several cases of the newly arrived scorpion stinging civilians have been reported and both the military and medical communities are said to be investigating.

Congress has scheduled hearings on the potential health and commercial threats posed by the newly arrived arthropod, but insiders warn that it is unlikely that funds to isolate and control the immigrant scorpions will be found in a budget already hard pressed to pay for the war and its unanticipated human side effects. Victims of the butcher scorpions will probably have to fend for themselves, sources said.

Reprinted from *The Thought,* November 1991

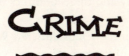

CRIME

◆ That there is such a thing as "truth serum," but because of the Fifth Amendment it cannot be used to gain confessions from criminals.

(So-called truth drugs are useful in gaining false confessions, as those who have been given them are most vulnerable to the power of suggestion.)

◆ That holding one's breath for random intervals enables one to outsmart a lie-detector machine; hardened criminals prefer a whiff of cocaine for insurance before their test.

(The best way to trick the machine is to be a pathological liar.)

◆ That the job of executioner is handed down from father to son, and that no one in the state save the prison warden knows his true identity.

- That condemned criminals bellow for a minister and convert the hour before they are put to death.
- That if you put tin foil in your hubcaps you will confuse police radar.
- That quicklime will destroy a corpse, and no self-respecting murderer should be without a supply of it.

(To quote from Philip Ward's Dictionary of Common Fallacies: "Some writers of detective stories still labor under the odd delusion that quicklime will 'eat' a dead body, even though it helped to convict the multiple murderess Mrs. Belle Gunness of La Porte, Indiana, whose fourteen victims were excellently preserved in the telltale substance.")

- That the dons of organized crime are careful to ensure that outside "civilians" are never harmed in mob wars.
- That we are winning—or beginning to—the war on drugs.
- That the reason the government has never *really* gone to work on the Mafia is because of the work the mob did for Uncle Sam during World War II.
- That every slice of pizza you eat puts seven cents into the hands of the Mafia, although no one is exactly sure of the routing of this money and the economics of the particular sum cited.
- That the Mafia in the 1920s declared Washington, D.C., an "off-limits" city for organized crime to avoid attracting attention to itself; that the crime rate among members of Congress themselves makes the Mafia's nonpresence moot.
- That the Mafia has secret holds on certain members of Congress and the judiciary that enable it to subvert governmental processes.
- That there is no justice as satisfying as when a lenient judge is mugged or burglarized by the very kind of person he is always letting off easily.
- That fingerprints are commonly taken from the handles of revolvers and used to catch murderers.

(In real life this rarely happens. It is, however, common in fiction.)

- That mass murderers always impressed their neighbors and elementary-school teachers as nice, quiet boys with good manners.

◆ That the most horrible crimes are committed by those on the lowest and uppermost levels of society.

◆ That the two easiest ways to acquire a vast sum of money in America are to engage in the smuggling of drugs or the bilking of the Medicaid system.

◆ That the police are never there when you need them, but always there when you go ten miles per hour over the limit.

◆ That a member of the Masonic order has never been hanged in the United States.

◆ That ground glass is an effective murder weapon.

(Unlike splintered glass, which is deadly, ground glass is virtually harmless. The authors of The Prevalence of Nonsense *report that the seventeenth-century physician Sir Thomas Browne proved the point by giving a dog "above a dram thereof, subtilly powdered in Butter and Paste, without any visible disturbance.")*

◆ That you cannot be accused of murder unless the body—the corpus delicti—is found.

(A number of murderers have been convicted after burning or otherwise disposing of their victims. Much of the confusion arises from the belief that the word "corpus" in corpus delicti refers to the corpse of the victim. The word actually refers to the body of the crime—i.e., proof that a crime has been committed.)

◆ That the eyes of the victim of a particularly vile murder will retain the image of the murderer.

◆ That the police always arrest or ticket the out-of-state driver.

◆ That the police enjoy going to private homes to settle disputes between a husband and wife because they are naturally nosy and can't wait to tell everyone what happened when they get back to the station.

◆ That from time to time a counterfeiter comes along whose work is so good that the U.S. government does not prosecute for fear of shaking confidence in paper money.

◆ That if a criminal survives three successive attempts by electrocution or hanging, the authorities will either free the criminal or let him live the rest of his life in prison.

◆ That one can be fined or imprisoned for killing a praying mantis.

◆ That it is illegal (and perhaps immoral) for a consumer to remove furniture tags—especially those attached to mattresses.

(The tag law originated as a health measure to prevent the unrevealed resale of used mattresses and other stuffed material that might have been contaminated by earlier owners. Rest assured that you can remove a mattress tag without being hauled off to prison.

However, Garrison Keillor pointed out a few years back that the tag on your mattress is "your BED LICENSE and illegal removal of the tag will mean that any children conceived on that mattress will be illegitimate.")

◆ That the threadbare commercial fishermen hanging around their boats at local docks wear shabby clothes because they want to fool the Internal Revenue Service, but they actually are making a killing smuggling drugs on weekends.

◆ That from time to time a dishonest technician is able to instruct a computer to knock a few cents off all major financial transactions and has these pennies credited to his private account. The odd cents are never missed and within months the renegade computer technician has pocketed a million dollars and moved to Brazil.

(There have doubtless been a few cases like this, but the more sophisticated operators no longer satisfy themselves with pennies. In 1981 a Brazilian-born couple managed to siphon hundreds of thousands of dollars from a Washington, D.C., mutual fund and deposit the sum—by computer—in banks abroad. They were apprehended and convicted.)

◆ That the FBI invented fingerprinting.

(The first man to suggest fingerprints be used to identify criminals was Dr. Henry Fauds of England in 1880. In 1882, Sir Francis Galton, a noted English scientist, scientifically established the fact that no two fingerprints are alike.)

DEATH

~~~~~~

♦   That most deaths occur between the hours of two and six in the morning.

♦   That the recently deceased spent their next-to-last mortal week eating scores of dinners. This is evidenced by the number of people who say, "I can't believe he's dead. Just to think I had dinner with him last week."

♦   That certain presidents are doomed to die in office because of the curse of the Twenty-Year Cycle.

(Supposedly, a president elected in a year divisible by twenty is destined to die in office. Through the 1980 election, nine men had been so elected; of these, six died during the immediate term—Harrison, 1840; Lincoln, 1860; Garfield, 1880; McKinley, 1900; Harding, 1920, and Kennedy, 1960. A seventh, Franklin Roosevelt, was also elected in a divisible-by-twenty year; he died during the term to which he was elected in 1944.)

♦   That a howling dog is a sign of death.

♦   That if you are the first to leave after a funeral, you will be the next to die.

♦   That there are a number of documented cases in which a clock has stopped working when its owner died.

♦   That if you ever have the misfortune to be on a falling elevator, simply "jump" off of the floor the instant the elevator hits and you'll be spared.

♦   That a phantom hearse sometimes appears and then quickly disappears just before a person dies.

♦   That you drown when you go down for the third time.

♦   That at the moment of death there is an immediate loss of a tiny amount of weight.

♦   That you can tell if somebody is dead by looking into their eyes.

(Only on stage and in B movies.)

♦ That people with severe heart attacks die when their hearts "literally explode."

(If this were true, autopsies would reveal scattered fragments.)

DRINK

♦ That the best beer is brewed from mountain stream water.
♦ That the Japanese can drink infinitely more sake, Russians and Poles more vodka, Mexicans more tequila, than you can— and still stay sober.
♦ That people are often frozen, bitten by poisonous snakes, or thrown from cars, but survive because they are totally inebriated.
♦ That you can drink more highballs (tall watered drinks) than cocktails even if the amount of liquor in each is equal.
♦ That champagne produces the worst of all hangovers.
♦ That cheap jug wine will usually beat expensive imported wine in blind tastings. Ditto for plain club soda, which will top imported sparkling water.
♦ That vodka has no taste.
♦ That all vodka is the same, so you may as well go out and buy a cheap one.
♦ That moving men have learned how to get roaring drunk during a day's work without anyone ever seeing the bottle.
♦ That a single jigger of absinthe will either kill you or render you blind.
♦ That a single jigger of olive oil, consumed prefestivities, will keep you sober and upright for the evening.
♦ That twelve jiggers of beer, consumed in rapid succession, will render immobile even the most renowned of collegiate drinkers.
♦ That various American millionaire families such as the Fricks, the Mellons, and the Fords are still drinking up the wine stocks their forefathers laid in just before Prohibition.

◆   That those $10,000 bottles of wine sold at fancy auctions turn to vinegar once uncorked.

◆   That the Allied advance across Europe in the Second World War was delayed for weeks because troops stopped to "liberate" wine cellars.

◆   That the Mafia introduced 7-Up during Prohibition to encourage young women to drink whiskey.

◆   That actor Paul Newman is the only man in America who can drink twenty-four cans of beer daily and keep that kind of waistline.

◆   That from time to time an old wino is spotted with a tarnished Phi Beta Kappa key hanging from his ravaged body.

(This is often embellished with the testimony of someone who actually saw such a key. In one version, a family is driving in New York City and gets lost in the Bowery. An old derelict looms into view as the car stops for a red light. He cleans the windshield with a dirty old rag in hopes of getting a few coins from the driver. As he leans over to wipe the other side of the windshield, the key is pressed against the glass.)

◆   That it is somehow worse to see a completely drunken woman than a totally soused man.

◆   That the mixture of aspirin and Coca-Cola is (a) a powerful intoxicant, (b) a powerful aphrodisiac, but, either way, (c) can kill you.

◆   That if you put a tooth in a glass of Coca-Cola overnight, it will have dissolved by morning. That is also true of a nail or a penny.

(Many experiments have proven this false, including our friend Bob Skole, who in March 1982 had a tooth extracted that is still sitting in a bottle of Coke in his bathroom. Here is Skole's report on the experiment, dated January 15, 1993, more than ten years later: "I still have the thing in Coke, now for 10 years, and the tooth is healthier than ever, with a lovely patina. [It costs a fortune to keep the cup filled with Coke, but it's all for the sake of science, and a possible Nobel Prize.]")

There are so many stories about Coca-Cola in circulation that the neologism "Cokelore" is used in folklore journals to refer to the phenomenon. These range from a host of fables having to do with foreign objects found in Coke bottles (in many of these the finder is offered vast sums in out-of-court settlements) to fanciful stories about the ends to which the company goes to protect its secret formula. In his *Dictionary of Misinformation* Tom Burnam tells of the popular myth in which the company is allowed to leap suddenly from a small operation to a multimillion-dollar international corporation. According to this story, back in the days when Coke was sold only at soda fountains, a man came to the officers of the company and told them that for $500 he would reveal the secret of untold corporate riches. He was given the $500 and announced the secret: "Bottle it!"

The word "coke," of course, has another connotation in the narcotics world, and the lore about Coca-Cola and cocaine is based in historic fact. According to H. L. Mencken's *American Language,* Supplement I, the name Coca-Cola is based on the names of two of the drink's constituents. It was registered as a trademark in 1893, and the company spent much money and legal effort fending off infringers who contrived soundalike names for their soft drinks (as in "Koke Cola"). Here is relevant language from the U.S. Supreme Court decision in Coca-Cola Company vs. Koke Company of America:

Before 1900 the beginning of the good will [of Coca-Cola] was more or less helped by the presence of cocaine, a drug that, like alcohol or caffeine or opium, may be described as a deadly poison or as a valuable item of the pharmacopoeia according to the rhetorical purposes in view.

The amount seems to have been very small, but it may have been enough to begin a bad habit, and after the Food and Drug Act of June 30, 1906, if not earlier, long before this suit was brought, it was eliminated from the plaintiff's compound. Coca leaves still are used, to be sure, but after they have been subjected to a drastic process that removes from them every characteristic substance except a little tannin and still less chlorophyll. The cola nut, at best, on its side furnishes but a very small portion of caffeine, which is now the only element that has appreciable effect. [254 U.S. 143; 65 L. Ed. 189]

As Mencken noted, "After cocaine was eliminated altogether from the formula, and the alarms about it began to subside, the company found the abbreviation coke a good advertisement, and has since stressed it in its advertising." The word *coke* "in the sense of a non-alcoholic drink made of vegetable extractives is now the property of the Coca-Cola Company."

EDUCATION

◆   That teachers in private schools took only academic courses in college and thus were not contaminated by pedagogical courses; the reverse is true for teachers in public schools.

◆   That if you had been given the money to fund four years in college when you were eighteen, and invested it in the stock market, you wouldn't have to work for a living now.

(Such computations can be made to work only when they allow that you were smart enough to buy IBM and Xerox at two bits a share and sold them when they hit their highs. A new myth may be developing in which you buy IBM at the high and short it for two years.)

◆   That there is no idea that is so farfetched that it is not believed and advocated by at least six professors and a handful of California psychologists.

◆   That it's important to repeat if you want someone to remember what you say. That it's important to repeat if you want someone to remember what you say.

◆   That children learn much faster than adults and that it is futile for a person to try to learn anything really new after his fortieth birthday.

◆   That memorizing something complex will improve your "memory power."

◆   That for all the aptitude testing done by companies, the armed forces, and educational institutions, no relationship has been demonstrated between later success and test scores (Stanines, GREs, LSATs, DATs, MCATs, College Boards, et cetera).

◆   That the study of mathematics develops a more logical mind.

◆   That no man is truly educated until he has read the Bible.

(A once reasonable thought, but one that has been stated solemnly so many times that it has become the crustiest of clichés.)

◆   That the better educated are necessarily of better character.

◆   That a teacher who arrives early for work shows enthusiasm and industry.

◆   That a teacher who stays late is a nut.

◆   That college professors need those four months off each year just to keep abreast of the scholarship in their field and recharge their batteries.

◆   That wives of teachers often think their husbands are talking down to them.

◆   Those who can, do. Those who can't, teach. Those who can't teach, teach teachers.

◆   That if one's college roommate dies during the school year, one's tuition for the year is complimentary.

FAMOUS PEOPLE

◆   That showman P. T. Barnum actually said, "There's a sucker born every minute."

(This from The Houston Post *of May 9, 1991: "On the 100th anniversary of the death of P. T. Barnum, Robert Pelton, curator of the Barnum Museum in Bridgeport, Connecticut, reveals that P.T. never uttered the phrase 'There's a sucker born every minute.' What he said was: 'The bigger the humbug, the better the people will like it.' Adding further insight was A. H. Saxon, who edited a 350-page book,* Selected Letters of P. T. Barnum, *with Columbia University Press in 1983. The line came from a publicist but Barnum was content to let it stand as a reasonable approximation of what he*

thought of his customers. In other words, Barnum believed that there was a sucker born every minute, he just never said it.")

◆ That Humphrey Bogart said, "Play it again, Sam"; that Charles Boyer said, "Come with me to the Casbah"; and that James Cagney delivered the line "You dirty rat" in a film.

◆ That if it had not been for Elizabeth Taylor, Richard Burton would have been the greatest actor in the English-speaking world.

◆ That Fidel Castro worked as a Hollywood extra in the early 1940s.

◆ That when Mayor Cermack of Chicago who shot while sitting next to President-elect Franklin D. Roosevelt, he said, "Better me than you, Mr. President," and then died.

(Cermack died a month later of colitis. The quote was made up by a newspaperman.)

◆ That Betty Crocker and Sara Lee were not only real people but first-class cooks.

(Betty Crocker was fictitious. Sara Lee, however, was real, and eight years old when her father, Charles Lubin, started the company, based in Deerfield, Illinois, which is known formally as The Kitchens of Sara Lee.)

◆ That Humphrey Bogart served as the model for the Gerber baby.

(The baby food was put on the market in 1928, when Bogy was twenty-nine years old.)

◆ That Walter Cronkite would make an infinitely better president, senator, or astronaut than anyone he has ever interviewed on television.

◆ That Thomas Dewey would have been elected president if he had not looked like a paper doll.

◆ That John Dillinger had an enormous member, which has been preserved and is now kept under lock and key in a dusty corner of the Smithsonian.

(Another version of this, preferred by those who "know" Washington, is that Dillinger's privates are to be found in formaldehyde in a jar at the Armed Forces Medical Museum, which is on the grounds of the Walter Reed Army Medical Center on Sixteenth Street. An intrepid reporter from the monthly Washington Tribune *actually went out to check on this story. It was not on public view, and he was too*

embarrassed to ask the curator if it was there. "Hell, I don't get paid enough to go out on a limb like that," wrote the reporter, Michael Leccese, in a moment of deep journalistic candor.)

◆ That Walt Disney had himself frozen, to be thawed when a cure was found for cancer.

(Disney was cremated on December 17, 1966.)

◆ That a lonely, gargantuan Mama Cass Elliott, 220 pounds, choked to death on a ham sandwich she was too tired to chew.

(This is one of the most popular rock myths, but as Joanna Powell of The Houston Post *found on investigating the rumor and reported in the paper's July 29, 1992, issue: ". . . the former lead singer of the Mamas and the Papas was not felled by a sandwich. A week after her death in London a coroner ruled that the 33-year-old had died of a heart attack. No food blocked her throat, and though she sometimes indulged, no alcohol or drugs were in her blood.")*

◆ That Albert Einstein had a terrible record as a student in math and physics.

(Walter Sullivan reported in The New York Times, *February 14, 1984: "Contrary to a popular legend that has given comfort to countless slow starters, young Albert Einstein was remarkably gifted in mathematics and excelled in physics, academic records recently acquired from Swiss archives show.")*

◆ That the Amy Fisher television movies prove this country is morally bankrupt.

◆ That Warren G. Harding was our worst President.

◆ That the man who languished in Spandau Prison in West Germany until his recent death was not really Rudolf Hess.

(According to those who believed in a Hess conspiracy, he escaped Germany in 1945, flew to Paraguay in a borrowed glider, and his place in prison was taken by his perfect double, Klaus von Spangenberg. Hess allegedly operated—or still operates—a flying school in Asunción, Paraguay.)

◆ That Sherlock Holmes was a real person.

◆ That Herbert Hoover was probably a better president than granted by historians, but he didn't know how to handle the media.

◆ That within hours of J. Edgar Hoover's death, President Nixon had troops seize the FBI director's infamous "personal files" and transport them to San Clemente. In due course

Nixon intends to use this material to blackmail his way back into politics.

♦ That Howard Hughes really fooled us all, and that in ten years or so he will reappear and regain his empire; he was flash-frozen by an unknown California scientist and is being stored in a vault in the West in a state of suspended animation.

♦ That David Janssen was the illegitimate son of Clark Gable.

♦ That Elton John and Olivia Newton-John were once married.

♦ That the small set of initials, *JS*, immediately below FDR's head on the Roosevelt dime stand for Josef Stalin and appear there through some sinister political plot.

(This belief grew in the months following the debut of the new dime in early 1946. The JS stands for artist John Sinnock. The Treasury Department was finally required to issue an official denial of the Stalin charge.)

♦ That the marking at the base of John F. Kennedy's neck on the fifty-cent piece is a hammer and sickle—perhaps put there by the same invisible hand that put *JS* on the dime.

♦ That JFK had been married once before he married Jackie.

(Although the tale is not nearly as prevalent as it was before the 1960 election, there are still people who believe that this was one of the major cover-ups of the twentieth century.)

♦ That Nikita Khrushchev was a playful bear and that the highlight of his life was his visit to Disneyland.

♦ That although General Douglas MacArthur was sort of a nut, his accomplishments nonetheless made him a valuable soldier.

(MacArthur was renowned for a preening ego that prompted him to demand personal credit for all triumphs in his command, regardless of his role. MacArthur tolerated neither dissent nor criticism.)

♦ That MacArthur delayed his arrival in the Philippines until he was assured that newsreel cameras were present to record his "I Shall Return" march through the surf; no Japanese soldier was within miles.

♦ That while playing for the Dallas Cowboys, Don Meredith was secretly married to both Tom Landry's daughter and ex–Cleveland Browns football coach Blanton Collier's daughter.

◆ That Sir Isaac Newton was beaned by an apple, which led him to wrap up his laws of gravity.

◆ That Richard Nixon will one day be viewed as a great president.

◆ That Richard Nixon was able to open relations with Red China because of, not despite, his Republican, anticommunist background. If Hubert Humphrey or George McGovern had tried it, the American people would not have stood for such a "sellout."

◆ That Ronald Reagan was the first choice for the role of Rick in *Casablanca*.

(This has been labeled a myth by USA Today, *which printed that it grew from an item long ago planted in* The Hollywood Reporter *to gain publicity for the film.)*

◆ That the day when Ronald (six letters) Wilson (six letters) Reagan (six letters) was elected to the presidency the number winning the Maryland lottery was 666 and many did not collect their winnings because it was the number of the devil.

◆ That Alfred Nobel was so conscience-stricken about his explosives inventions that he wanted to promote peace, and thus left his estate to found the Nobel prizes.

(Actually, in the years immediately prior to his death at the turn of the century, he owned Bofors, one of Europe's most famous makers of artillery and heavy cannon, used by all sides in World Wars I and II, and countless other wars. Some peacemonger.)

◆ That FDR sold us down the river at Yalta.

◆ That one of the judges that Roosevelt tried to pack the Supreme Court with didn't have a law degree.

(Such an appointment would have done no harm to the U.S. Constitution or federal law; neither requires that a federal judge at any level be an attorney.)

◆ That Colonel Jacob Ruppert—the Yankees' owner in the early days—came up with the girth-disguising pinstripe uniform when Babe Ruth joined the Yankees from the Boston Red Sox in 1920.

(A number of people have dealt with this one, including Parade *magazine, which ran this rebuttal in its April 5, 1992, issue: "The trouble with this story is that the famous Yankee pinstripes made their debut in 1912—when George Herman Ruth was just 17 and still a*

somewhat slim, left-handed catcher for St. Mary's Industrial School for Boys in Baltimore, where he also pitched and sometimes even played third base.")

◆ That a poor immigrant boy came to America and grew to love the country so that he added USA to his name of John Philipso and went on to become John Philip Sousa, the eminent composer and band director.

◆ That Adlai Stevenson did *not* become president because of his wit and finely tuned sense of humor.

◆ That Willie Sutton robbed banks "because that was where the money was."

("I never said it," Sutton stated in his memoir. "The credit belongs to some enterprising reporter who apparently felt a need to fill out his copy." But Sutton liked the phrase so much he entitled his memoir Where the Money Was.)

◆ That a major reason why Robert A. Taft failed in three attempts to get the Republican presidential nomination was his unfortunate set of initials (which would have provided a succession from FDR to HST to RAT).

◆ That William Tell once shot an apple off his son's head with his crossbow.

◆ That George Washington had wooden teeth.

(His teeth were actually made of ivory.)

◆ That a young George Washington threw a silver dollar across the Potomac or, as some versions have it, the Rappahannock.

(Start with this. Silver dollars were not minted in Colonial America and though there are narrow spots on the Rappahannock, there are none on the Potomac.)

◆ That George Washington stood up in a rowboat crossing the Delaware on Christmas Eve 1776.

(Only so in paintings. This is absurd on its face. Washington would have been an easy target for British sharpshooters and would not have stood in a small boat in cold waters unless he wanted to tip it over and kill all aboard, including himself.)

◆ That Lawrence Welk once said on his show, "And now here's a little ditty from World War Eye!" (I = eye).

(That Welk repeatedly denied this simply added an air of credibility.)

◆ That great historical figures required very little sleep.
◆ That a number of prominent Americans have been secret members of the Ku Klux Klan.
◆ That most great men and women were born of poor but honest parents.

THREE W. C. FIELDS MYTHS

• That Uncle Claude's tombstone contains the inscription "All things considered, I'd rather be in Philadelphia." Actually, Fields has no tombstone. He was cremated—at his behest—on June 3, 1949, some thirty months after his death; his ashes repose in niche 20805 of the Columbarium of Nativity, The Great Mausoleum, Forest Lawn Memorial Park, Glendale, California. The oft-repeated quotation was given by Fields to a writer for *Vanity Fair* magazine in 1937 who asked movie stars what inscription they would choose for their gravestones.

• That Uncle Claude, in a self-description, said, "No man who hates dogs and children can be all bad." Comedians take material where it can be found. In this instance, the remark apparently was uttered by Byron Darnton of *The New York Times,* after listening to a bore at a cocktail party. The bon mot got into print in *Harper's* magazine in 1930, attributed to Darnton.

• That Uncle Claude so distrusted the world of finance that he opened bank accounts in numerous institutions under assumed names, often in the company of his boon companion John Barleycorn, and was unable to remember them later. Consequently, he lost scores of thousands of dollars. To the contrary, according to testimony at a hearing on the probate of his will, Fields was a painstaking records-keeper, for he listed no less than twenty-three separate bank accounts he opened between 1903 and 1946, the year he died.

(Will Fowler, the California writer who discovered martinis at Fields's knee at age thirteen, in the company of father Gene Fowler, gently dispels these Fields stories in his The Second Handshake, Lyle Stuart, Inc., Secaucus, NJ, 1980. *Fowler avows that the "tombstone" legend is regularly repeated on TV talk shows by "Fields experts"*

whose portfolios consist of "a sheet of the comedian's personal stationery with a letter addressed to another person.")

FASHION

◆ That women's and, increasingly, men's fashions are con-
trolled by a small clique with foreign accents. This clique has
a mysterious lock on every department-store buyer in America.
◆ That women's clothes are designed by men who hate
women.
◆ That hunters should wear red for safety.
*(The National Safety Council says that fluorescent orange is bet-
ter, especially at dawn and dusk, when red is hard to see.)*
◆ That only older men wear boxer shorts.
◆ That rats are systematically bred in South African sewers,
made into fur coats, and exported to the United States disguised as mink, ermine, and seal.
*(This story was picked up by the Associated Press from the Johan-
nesburg Star and appeared in a number of American newspapers before
it was discovered to be a 1980 April Fools' joke. Retractions notwith-
standing, the story continues to make the rounds as fact verified by the
AP. One editor wrote of his paper: "The cynical, sharp-eyed, suspicious wire-desk editors at the St. Petersburg Times bought the story
hook, line, and sinker.")*
◆ That red flannel is warmer than white.
◆ That underneath their habits, all nuns are bald.
◆ That women dress for other women rather than for men.
◆ That ashes are good for carpets, especially cigar ashes.
◆ That the color of pea soup is good for the eyes and spirit,
which is why the bulkheads of Navy ships, the innards of the

Pentagon, and most of the walls in civilian government agencies are painted in this bilious green.

◆ That wearing hats causes premature baldness.

Fill in the Blanks

A collection of credos that take on different nouns at different times and places.

◆ That _____ is not really dead, but survives in a coma in a heavily guarded hospital room in _____.

(Perhaps the commonest version has John F. Kennedy in a coma at Parkland Hospital, where Jacqueline Onassis still secretly visits him once a month, but it is also applied to other popular figures ranging from James Dean to John Lennon.)

◆ That money donated to _____ is covertly channeled into paying for _____.

(One version of this, which circulated a few years ago, had the March of Dimes supporting the abortion of fetuses suspected of having birth defects.)

◆ That free speech is a fine thing but that it has been taken too far in the case of _____, who should be brought under control.

◆ That because an engineer once misplaced a decimal point, a large, brand-new _____ collapsed.

◆ That the major oil companies are repressing the technology that would allow the conversion of plentiful, inexpensive _____ into a source of energy.

◆ That the world is divided into two classes of people; those who _____ and those who don't.

◆ That if all the money that has been spent by Americans on _____ had been applied to the problem of _____, the problem would be solved by now.

◆ That we can put men on the moon, yet we can't even _____.

◆ That a group of hoodlums called the _____ Rats terrorized the streets of _____ during the forties and fifties/fifties and sixties/sixties and seventies.

(If all the stories of the Rats were true, they would have overpowered the U.S. Armed Forces at peak strength. A common epilogue tacked onto the Rats story is that the members are grown up, have children of their own, and are respected members of the community.)

◆ That the _____ house at _____ College/ University was the model for the movie *Animal House.*

◆ That _____ was the model for *Dr. Strangelove.*

(There are many Strangeloves, but the most commonly cited are Herman Kahn, Henry Kissinger, and Wernher von Braun.)

◆ That _____ is exactly like what happened to cause the fall of Rome. _____ is just like what went on in Nazi Germany.

◆ That if you collect enough _____ they can be exchanged for a kidney dialysis machine.

(This is a cruel credo that causes the National Kidney Foundation to be occasionally given mountains of cigarette wrappers, box tops, tea bag envelopes, or whatever.)

◆ That if you give a _____ one drink of hard liquor, he'll drink the whole bottle.

(Said of Germans by Swedes, Danes by Germans, et cetera.)

◆ That the main ingredient of _____ is sugar.

◆ That the Red Cross charges the going rate or more for _____ during major disasters and World Wars.

(The blank in this amazingly virulent untruism can be filled with coffee, doughnuts, sandwiches, or blood. Red Cross villainy of this sort was a part of the folklore of World War II—along with the completely unfounded belief that the Red Cross was charging GIs in Iceland high prices for sweaters that were knitted by American volunteers—and hangs on to this day. In 1961 the DAV Magazine, *published by the Disabled American Veterans, carried an editorial attacking the doughnut myth, which said in part: "Like so many such stories this one has faded from reality to legend. It's sort of like having been chewed out by Patton . . . or having to eat spoiled field rations . . . or drinking hair tonic strained through bread. We all did it. You just aren't anyone who was anyone if you didn't have to pay for your Red Cross donuts during World War II."*

A few years ago one of the coauthors of this book was interviewing Red Cross President George M. Elsey, and the subject of the organization's never-ending campaign to spike the coffee, sandwich, and doughnut rumor came up. "Not long ago," he said, "I appeared on a television show in Hawaii on which viewers were allowed to call in and ask me questions. An irate man called in to charge that we had sold sandwiches when Agnes brought heavy flooding to Elmira, New York, which, as always, was not true.")

♦   That some time ago a _____ with an experimental engine was accidentally sold to an unsuspecting consumer who was bowled over when he found it got 125 miles to the gallon. The mistake was discovered, and the man was paid a vast sum for the car and his silence.

(What is never made clear about this story is why Mazda, VW, Ford, GM, or whoever is holding this development back when it could, in fact, give the company an overwhelming sales advantage.

Could it be the dark hand of the oil companies?)

♦   That we're winning the war on _____.

FOOD

♦   That honey is less fattening than sugar.

♦   That Perrier is a better thirst-quencher than either water or ordinary soda, and better for your health at that.

♦   That Howard Johnson's once had good food.

♦   That it's just as well that we do not know the true contents of hot dogs sold by sidewalk vendors.

♦   That if you befriend the maître d' of a small French restaurant and exchange a few words in French with him each time you enter, the chef will ensure that you are served the best chop from the kitchen, and a bottle of wine "reserved for our best customers" will be offered to you. But be prepared to pay a tip of at least 25 percent if you want a table the next time you visit, and don't examine the label on the wine bottle too closely.

◆ That there is an American Heart Association diet that permits one to eat hot dogs and ice cream and lose weight.

(Bob Levey investigated this in his May 20, 1988, Washington Post *column and reported that the "American Heart Association Diet" is a fraud. Christy Passmore, a spokeswoman at AHA headquarters in Dallas, says the "AHA Diet" crops up somewhere in the country once every six months or so. The AHA has no idea who starts it, or restarts it. Nor can the AHA do much to prevent the starts and restarts, since anyone can type AHA at the top of a piece of paper without bothering to obtain approval.)*

◆ That a roadside restaurant with many trucks parked outside is ipso facto a good place to eat.

◆ That the only proper way to judge barbecue joints is by the number of pickup trucks outside.

◆ That a good way to determine whether or not a Chinese restaurant is any good is to see if many Orientals are eating there. If there are only non-Orientals dining, chances are that the food is not very good.

◆ That Chinese food might fill you up for the moment, but you'll be hungry again long before the next mealtime.

(Not exactly so, according to gastroenterologist Dr. Basil Lucak of the New York University Medical Center. In an interview with The New York Times *published October 5, 1984, Dr. Lucak said, "There is little, if any, scientific evidence that proves anyone gets hungry an hour or two after completing a Chinese meal."*

Persons might feel satiated at first because "foods which are high in bulk, such as grains, vegetables, fruits, and fibers fill up the stomach and cause distention." The easing of this distention causes a sense of hunger rather than actual hunger.)

◆ That in order for a deli to be any good: (1) the waiters must be thoroughly obnoxious, and (2) at least one very fat man with a pinkie ring must be seated and eating near the front door.

◆ That restaurants make all their money on booze and lose or break even on food no matter how it is priced.

◆ That when a new fast-food outlet opens, it will serve oversized hamburgers and give you at least a dozen extra fries for the first few weeks, but will then cut back to normal portions.

♦ That recipes for commercial chocolate chip cookies are bought and sold for extravagant prices.

(This disclaimer appeared on a bag of Mrs. Fields cookies:

Mrs. Fields recipe has never been sold. There is a rumor circulating that the Mrs. Fields Cookie recipe was sold to a woman at a cost of $250.00. A chocolate chip cookie recipe was attached to the story. I would like to tell all my customers that the story is not true, this is not my recipe and I have never sold the recipe to anyone. Mrs. Fields recipe is a delicious trade secret.

Sincerely,

Debbi Fields)

♦ That twenty years ago railroad dining cars routinely served food that surpassed in quality that of any three-star restaurant in France; the dining-room waiter, while serving this feast, would deliver a witty monologue on the history and customs of the countryside through which the train was passing; that by custom, passed down from one's father, his name was always George.

♦ That anything that is baked, fried, or put up in jars always tastes better if it is done in the country than in a city or suburb.

♦ That food tastes better when consumed outdoors.

♦ That there was a Golden Age of natural goodness when food was richer, firmer, and better-tasting. This took place before the age of preservatives, additives, and agribusiness, but after the earlier age of adulteration that led to the Food and Drug Act.

♦ That hot food is more nourishing than cold food and that one should have at least one hot meal a day.

♦ That hot beverages will quench your thirst faster than cold ones.

♦ That oysters are good only in months with the letter *r* in them.

♦ That most of the scallops you get in restaurants are actually cut from shark or skate and made to look like scallops.

◆ That you shouldn't shop for groceries when you're hungry.

(Why not? It can be argued that a hungry shopper, armed with some nutritional and dietary information, is a good shopper. Should you not shop for a coat when you are chilly?)

◆ That people from Texas are so jaded by conventional chili recipes that they are eager to try varieties from such places as Aurora, Illinois, that incorporate such features as dark olives and bell peppers. Rank chauvinism demands that Texans darken and glower when the dish appears, so the cook should not feel slighted.

◆ That the best chili is to be found in restaurants with the decor of a bus-station waiting room in San Antonio, Texas.

◆ That ice cream, apple pie, and soda pop are American discoveries.

(Ice cream as we know it today was created in Europe—probably England, maybe Italy. Americans popularized apple pie but it was first enjoyed in Europe. Carbonated drinks developed on both sides of the Atlantic, and the word "pop" for such a beverage almost certainly came from Britain, where it imitated the sound of a cork coming out of a bottle.)

◆ That you can't buy a good steak in Texas. Or Chicago. Or Kansas City. They are all "sent east" to the big restaurants. This is also true of the best Maine lobster, which goes west, and the best Columbia salmon, which migrates east.

(There are many other versions of this belief. Peter McAlevey, an editor at Inside Sports *magazine, tells us, "Some years back while in college, I was traveling through the backwaters of Mexico, searching for experience [as students are wont to do]. Eschewing the beaten path, I found myself one evening drinking in a Mexican workers' bar in an unnamed small town near the Arizona border. After my third or fourth strong-but-awful-tasting taste of tequila, I happened to inquire of one of the drinking workers where I could purchase some of the good tequila I'd heard so much about. [The stuff they drink there is real p*** water.] Turning to me he replied, in broken English, 'Good tequila? Yes, I had good tequila once . . . in Wisconsin!' " Summation: The Mexican credo in play here appears to be a corollary to the American credo that one can't get a good steak in Kansas City—to wit, that all good tequila is shipped to the wealthier United States market.)*

◆ That a person has to be born in Mississippi to eat possum stew and keep it down.

◆ That it is wrong and unhealthful to consume either milk and pickles or milk and shellfish at the same sitting.

◆ That the word "sex'" is baked into the surface of Ritz Crackers.

(This was "discovered" in a 1976 book, Media Sexploitation. *It is nonsense. Look for yourself.)*

◆ That fish is brainfood.

(The public has been swallowing this whopper for decades without one scintilla of scientific evidence.)

◆ That the most outwardly rigid devotees of natural foods occasionally sneak a Twinkie, Devil Dog, or fistful of Pringle's.

◆ That corn bread should never be cut with a knife, but should be broken.

◆ That antifreeze is a common ice-cream ingredient.

(The ice cream industry has fought this falsehood for years; but the battle has been made tougher by the fact that the ice cream industry has also fought having to list ingredients on its packages. The absurdity of the credo is evident: Why would anyone put antifreeze in a frozen product?)

◆ That chocolate is addictive, causes pimples, promotes tooth decay, and in certain cases acts as an aphrodisiac.

◆ That one is expected to sample the wares when food shopping.

(Customers in supermarkets who munch on grapes, loose food, or shelled nuts don't think they're stealing. They justify their behavior by thinking of it as quality control or sampling. Store personnel call such people "grazers.")

◆ That the medically proper thing to do when you have swallowed a fish bone is to eat bread.

◆ That certain types of junk foods are impregnated with secret chemicals that act as "appetite aphrodisiacs," making the eater unable to stop after a sensible amount of munching.

◆ That red M&Ms have aphrodisiacal qualities, which is why they are so hard to find.

◆ That green M&Ms have aphrodisiacal qualities, which is why naughty-minded boys slip them to high school girlfriends on Saturday-night dates.

(Wendy Jaffee, an entrepreneurial-minded lawyer-lady from Northridge, California, capitalized on this persistent myth in 1991 by starting a candy company, Cool Chocolate, Inc., to produce M&M clones which she sold as "The Green Ones." Mars, Inc., which manufactures "the real M&Ms," didn't think much of the idea and sued her for trademark infringement and unfair competition. Ms. Jaffee promptly donned a scanty outfit and struck a revealing pose for People *magazine, lolling on a bed covered with Green Ones and saying, "They send a definite signal." She told* The National Law Journal, *"They make you horny." She also went on the TV show "Studs" and dated two bachelors, only one of whom was allowed to try "The Green Ones" to make the evening . . . ah, more interesting. Jaffee told* People, *"He was definitely the steamier date." Jaffee also claimed that a color therapist told her that green stimulates sexual activity. Perhaps, but a 1950s-era myth held that male homosexuals signaled their sexual preference by wearing the color green, an erroneous assertion that one might choose not to repeat at a St. Patrick's Day parade.*

U.S. District Judge Garrett E. Brown, Jr., of Trenton, sided with Mars, Inc. The National Law Journal *reported on December 14, 1992, that he signed an order restraining Jaffee from marketing the candies in their incarnation as M&Ms.*

Red M&Ms, which some teenagers insisted also had aphrodisiacal value, vanished from the market in 1976, prompting reports that parents insisted that they no longer be sold since they were leading to sexual promiscuity in schools. In fact, the reds were withdrawn after the federal government banned Red Dye No. 2 as a suspected carcinogen. Although the Mars Company used Red Dye Nos. 3 and 4 for the candies, it withdrew the red M&Ms to avoid consumer confusion. Mars quietly put them back on the market during the 1986 Christmas season. Helping to get the reds back on the market was a Knoxville, Tennessee, photographer named Paul Hethmon, who created the Society for the Preservation and Restoration of Red M&M's and got other candy lovers to write the company. When the reds came back, M&M/Mars sent Hethmon a letter saying, "Good things happen to those who wait.")

◆ That brown M&Ms are an antidote to the nastier colors.
◆ That brown eggs are more nutritious than white ones. Also, that eggs consumed on a farm are vastly superior to those bought in a store.

(The ageless line that the visitor must utter when having farm eggs: "You know, it's impossible to get eggs like this in the city.")

◆ That the smell of a pink or green chemical mouthwash is less offensive than that of garlic.

◆ That ripe blueberries attract venomous snakes.

(A belief no doubt fostered by blueberry-patch owners.)

◆ That banquet food is by definition bad and composed of rubber chicken, pebblelike peas, and wilted salad.

◆ That if a drinking glass is ever used to hold gasoline, the taste will remain no matter how many times the vessel is washed.

◆ That cane sugar is sweeter than beet sugar.

◆ That tea is more healthful than coffee.

◆ That eating green apples will cause a terrible stomach ache.

◆ That eating carrots improves your vision.

(The published response of the American Academy of Ophthalmology: "It is true that carrots are rich in Vitamin A, which is essential for sight; however, many other foods also contain Vitamin A. Only a small amount is necessary for vision. A well-balanced diet, with or without carrots, provides all the Vitamin A necessary for good vision.")

◆ That an apple a day keeps the doctor away.

◆ That the addition of cottage cheese and a pear half to a meal reduces its caloric total.

(This belief comes from the custom of dieters' specials, which offer a regular entrée with regular cottage cheese as a sop to those who believe that regular cottage cheese is a lo-cal option.)

◆ That when you are told there will be a twenty-minute wait for a table and would-you-like-to-wait-in-the-bar, you can expect to have time for three drinks before your name is called.

◆ That the French developed their famous sauces to cover up the flavor of the sewer rats that they were forced to eat during the Great Famine, the Revolution, the Dark Ages, and following the Battle of Agincourt.

◆ That impulse buys in supermarkets are at eye level. So if you want to save money you have to reach up or down.

(This is probably true at the checkout counter, but not in the rest of the store. The business is highly competitive and stores feature sale items in the most prominent locations.)

♦ That one can gather nuts in May.

(Despite the line "Here we go gathering nuts in May," we could find none that fell so early in the year.)

♦ That most of the customers in health stores are hypochondriacs.

William Tammeus, columnist of the *Kansas City Star,* is a longtime credo-monger whose favorite beliefs come from a family source who has become such a font of conventional thought and superstition that he has named these beliefs for his mother-in-law's mother: "Gerti-isms." This is a collection of the best:

♦ Never tell a dream before breakfast unless you want it to come true.

♦ If a pin point is pointing toward you, pick it up—it is good luck.

♦ If you drop a piece of silverware on the floor you will have company before the day is over.

♦ If you drop your comb on the floor, step on it before you pick it up or you will have bad luck.

♦ Never rock an empty rocking chair—bad luck.

♦ Dream about water or babies—bad luck.

♦ Never walk under a ladder—bad luck.

♦ If you forget something when going away from home and go back to get it, sit down and count to ten before you leave again or you will have bad luck.

♦ When the leaves on a tree show their backsides, it is a sign of rain.

♦ When you see a sun dog (a rainbow around the sun) it is a sign of storms within a week.

♦ If water all boils away when you are cooking something there will be a storm.

♦ If the sun goes down behind a cloud it will be stormy the next day.

♦ Sing before breakfast—cry before sleep.

♦ It is bad luck to have a bird get in your house—someone in the family will die.

♦ If someone gives you a gift that is a sharp object (knife, pin, etc.) you must give them a penny or your friendship will end.

♦ In spring when you hear frogs singing for the first time it will freeze three times after that.

♦ When you dream of someone who is dead, the next day you will hear from or talk with someone you haven't heard from recently.

♦ If you say a person's name by mistake it means that person is thinking about you.

♦ If your ears ring, someone is talking about you.

♦ If your nose itches, you are going to get a letter or hear from a friend.

♦ If you go in one door and out another you will bring company to that house.

♦ When you see a fly in the house in the off-season it is a sign of warmer weather.

♦ If you take more food when you still have some of the same food left on your plate someone will come to your house hungry.

♦ Get out of bed on the same side you got in or you will have bad luck.

♦ If your corn hurts or a bone aches there will be a storm.

♦ Never open an umbrella in the house—bad luck.

♦ If you take stitches in something that a person is wearing, a lie will be told for each stitch taken.

♦ If you spill salt, toss some of it over your left shoulder or you will have bad luck.

♦ Break a mirror—seven years of bad luck.

♦ If the bottom of your foot itches you will walk on strange ground.

♦ If you have a scratch on your arm, the length of it will be the length of a trip you will take.

♦ If your left palm itches, someone is going to hand you

money; if your right palm itches, you are going to hand someone else money.

GOVERNMENT

◆   That the federal bureaucracy has purposely interpreted and enforced laws so as to undermine confidence in those laws.

(Popular mythology has it that devious bureaucrats have, for instance, discredited endangered-species acts by chasing elderly women in ancient fur coats rather than going after poachers and importers.)

◆   That government-assistance programs usually do more harm than good.

◆   That nothing is so simple that it can be accomplished efficiently by the government.

◆   That you cannot solve a problem by throwing money at it.

◆   That the statue atop the U.S. Capitol is that of a pregnant Indian woman and symbolizes the birth of the nation.

(It was revealed in The Washington Post *of October 3, 1977, that this myth was intentionally spread by Bob Sanders, a Capitol policeman, who told it to vast numbers of tourists.)*

◆   That the government sells Jeeps at auction every month in Arizona (or perhaps North Carolina) for $200 each, but friends and relatives of master sergeants have the market cornered.

◆   That people routinely overlooked by the nation's massive welfare system are the saddest and most needy, but that there is always room on the rolls for a glib loafer.

◆   That the infrastructure is crumbling.

◆   That in order to attract good people into government service you have to pay them higher wages than prevail in the private sector.

◆   That the national debt is no great problem because we owe it to ourselves.

◆   That there are bureaucrats in the federal government who have spent years in unmarked offices, doing not a lick of work during the day, their existence unknown even to their nominal superiors. They write novels, listen to the radio, and take four-hour lunch breaks while we taxpayers give them $35,000 a year.

◆ That key government officials know more about the Russians, the Mafia, and the Kennedys than the rest of us can ever hope to learn.

◆ That if we could only elect "the right people," government institutions would work just fine.

◆ That no matter how democratic a nation, its diplomats will always be highborn.

◆ That the government can "fine-tune" the economy by tinkering with the money supply.

◆ That if the Postal Service were entirely turned over to private enterprise it would become much more efficient.

◆ That a letter without a zip code will travel as quickly as or more quickly than one without. We put them on letters because we are told to do so.

◆ That you should be aware that the coded numbers that appear on the peel-off label on your federal tax form can trigger an audit.

◆ That there was never any gold at Fort Knox.

◆ That from time to time there is a case in which a child will murder his parents and then get government survivor benefits as an orphan.

(Remarkably, until a short time ago this was true. The Social Security Administration found that it had paid in two such cases in California. The loophole has presumably been closed, as Social Security officials have advised field offices not to process claims from "survivors who may have been involved in an intentional act which resulted in the death of a parent.")

◆ That the FBI has a master switchboard on Eighth Street, SE, or on New York Avenue in Washington, D.C. that permits agents to listen to any conversation on any telephone line in the world. Transcripts are computerized and fed into citizens' dossiers. Former Attorney General Ramsey Clark did not fire J. Edgar Hoover, because the FBI director knew, from his files, how many bottles of Shiner Beer Clark drank at a University of Texas fraternity house party in the 1940s.

♦ That if you build a house and don't put on front steps, it will be considered "unfinished," and you will not have to pay real estate taxes.

♦ That air-conditioning is responsible for the mushrooming of government and government regulations because it allowed legislators to stay in Washington for the summer.

♦ That there will be no new taxes and that when a politician of either party makes that promise, believe him or her.

♦ That government economists can predict economic trends rationally.

♦ That you can't fight city hall.

HEALTH AND MEDICINE

♦ That new miracle drugs of potentially great—perhaps revolutionary—benefit to humanity are being kept off the market by bureaucrats and regulators in Washington who are subjecting them to years of unneeded testing and bogging them down in tons of paperwork.

♦ That vast numbers of Americans die, within weeks, of physical examinations at which they were deemed to be in good health.

♦ That milk is good for ulcers.

(Milk is rich in protein, which stimulates acid production in the stomach and irritates an ulcer, says American Health Magazine.*)*

♦ That medical doctors know next to nothing about either nutrition or sex.

♦ That medical doctors must know Latin.

♦ That the comeuppance of modern medicine is that it has done nothing to cure the common cold.

- That coldness causes colds and that one should bundle up to avoid catching a cold.

(American Health Magazine *reported in 1991 that "repeated experiments indicate that people left shivering outdoors are no more likely to catch a cold than those who stay warm indoors." It should be pointed out that if this were true there would be no colds in warmer climates and Eskimos would be suffering all year long. Colds are produced by viruses.*)

- That all doctors have atrocious handwriting, which is a function of their frenzied note-taking in medical school.
- That all medical doctors play golf.

(*No less august an organization than the American Medical Association conducted a survey in 1979 to prove that a mere 11 percent of the nation's doctors play the game.*)

- That medical doctors are taught to write prescriptions in a secret code that only they and the druggist can understand.

(*They do not use standard abbreviations; but these are hardly secret. For instance, o.d. stands for every day and o.m. for every morning.*)

- That sponges used in surgery are frequently forgotten and left inside the patient. Each operating room has an attendant whose duty it is to record the passing of sponges, but he or she is frequently distracted. These omissions cause no problems for the negligent doctor, for at the insistence of the insurance companies a variety of sponge has been developed that cannot be detected by X rays. Hence malpractice suits are impossible.
- That brushing one's teeth with plain baking soda, or even salt, is a more effective antidote to tooth decay than those high-priced pastes.

(*True, if you are willing to dismiss all that has been shown to be true about fluoride and other decay-fighting chemicals.*)

- That there are no brave men in a dentist's office.
- That you should never open windows at night, as the night air causes disease.
- That a guy who claims that he is receiving radar signals in his head should be carted away for psychiatric examination.

(*Not so fast, caution three scientists who have studied the subject. In its December 1982 issue,* Psychology Today *summarized reports* by *Chung-Kawng Chou* and *Arthur W. Guy of the School of Medicine and College of Engineering of the University of Washington, and Robert Galambos of the School of Medicine of the University of California in San Diego. They reported that "human beings with normal high-frequency hearing can perceive an auditory sensation when exposed to microwave pulses of sufficient energy content," as happens when people are standing near a radar or microwave transmitter. The pulses might be heard as "clicks, buzzes, or hisses," the researchers wrote.*

Nonetheless, the first persons to report "hearing" radar signals "encountered skepticism and rather pointed questions about their mental health." What is now known is that microwave or radar signals cause an uneven heating of the head, setting up a thermoelastic pressure wave. As Psychology Today's *Frank Kendig summarized: "This wave is transmitted by the bones of the head to the inner ear. Moral: Don't disbelieve everything you hear.")*

◆ That excesses in lechery, rich food, and strong drink are the chief causes of gout, which most often afflicts men of exceptional talent and bank accounts.

◆ That sex will clear up acne.

◆ That wearing garlic around the neck protects the wearer from whatever epidemic is making the rounds.

◆ That going outside after washing your hair will cause pneumonia and possibly lead to your demise.

◆ That you should feed a cold and starve a fever.

(From an article on popular misconceptions in Family Safety *magazine: "This old saw [it goes back in some form or other to Roman times] has been repeatedly attacked but still crops up. One doctor who fought it asked that the phrase 'He fed fevers' be inscribed on his tombstone.")*

◆ That if you get frostbite, you should rub the injured area with snow.

(Today's favored remedy, according to the National Safety Council, is warm water, but never hot water.)

◆ That Americans have the best health care in the world.

◆ That Americans enjoy the best and healthiest diet in the world.

(The evidence suggests that our taste for fat is creating poor health.)

♦ That if you cross your eyes and the wind changes, they will stay that way.

(Folks who have enough muscular control to deliberately cross their eyes are probably least likely to be cross-eyed. The wind has nothing to do with being cross-eyed nor does the earth shifting on its axis.)

♦ That wearing a hat inside the house will cause you to get a headache.

♦ That a summer cold is more tenacious than a winter cold and will therefore hang on longer.

♦ That regularity—that is, a bowel movement at roughly the same time each day—is the right and healthy human condition.

♦ That sleeping outside increases your resistance to colds and other illnesses.

♦ That an enormous appetite is a symptom of having a tapeworm.

(As grotesque as they can be, morbid hunger is not a symptom of their presence.)

♦ That every time you hiccup it means that you are growing.

♦ That freezing kills germs.

(In 1926 The American Journal of Public Health reported on more than 100 public-health crises created by ice cream and the inescapable conclusion—known since the nineteenth century—was that freezing helped preserve rather than kill the germs that caused diphtheria, typhoid, and other illnesses.)

♦ That sleepwalkers are generally immune to harm.

♦ That if a grown man gets mumps, he will become sterile.

(John Camp reports in his Magic, Myth and Medicine *that a London hospital team studied 200 men who had mumps and could find no evidence of an inability to father.)*

♦ That swallowing seeds (watermelon seeds, for example) will cause appendicitis.

♦ That you should put nothing in your ear smaller than your elbow.

(This credo was created to forestall kids from putting sharp objects in their ears, but it rules out eardrops, Q-tips, and earplugs, to name a few.)

♦ That sea air is particularly good for your health.

◆ That it is possible to build up one's resistance to the common cold.

◆ That if you put your shoes under the bed you can rid yourself of nightmares.

◆ That unless you have a lamp on in the room, watching television will ruin children's eyes, as well as your own.

(This myth was created in the early 1950s by an innovative Philadelphia public relations man named J. Robert Mendte, on behalf of a client who manufactured lamps.)

◆ That reading in dim light can harm your eyes.

(Literature provided by the American Academy of Ophthalmology addresses this issue: "Using your eyes in dim light does not damage them. It wasn't too long ago that all nighttime reading and sewing was done by candlelight or with gas or kerosene lamps. However, good lighting does make reading easier and prevents eye fatigue, especially for those people who wear bifocals.")

◆ That frightful experiences or grief will cause one's hair to turn white overnight.

(This biological impossibility is often attributed to famous people. Marie Antoinette's hair turned during the night after she was told she would be put to death. Ripley's Believe It or Not Book of Americana, 1976, carried this item:

ANNIE OAKLEY
(1860–1926) FAMED AS A SHARPSHOOTER
WITH NERVES OF STEEL
WAS IN A RAILROAD ACCIDENT
NEAR WHEELING, W. VA.,
AND HER HAIR TURNED SNOW WHITE IN A FEW HOURS.)

◆ That you can cure hiccups by drinking a glass of water as fast as you can without stopping. Or by eating a tablespoon of sugar. Or by having someone jump out at you from behind a closet door, saying "BOO." Or by holding your breath for as long as you can. Or by drinking from the opposite side of a glass.

◆ That it is dangerous to swim for an hour after one has eaten. Eating causes debilitating stomach cramps.

(Physicians scoff at this belief; its chief utility seems to be that of giving parents a brief respite after lunch before returning to the beach with energetic children. Some canny parents insist on an hour and a half. It has been suggested, however, that swimming immediately after a heavy meal is not a good idea for adults at risk for a heart attack.)

◆ That the right brain is the seat of creativity.

(No scientific evidence for this. In healthy people the two hemispheres work together.)

◆ That wearing rubber overshoes inside the house can lead to a host of unspecified illnesses.

◆ That "cellulite" is different from, and therefore more excusable than, plain old ordinary fat.

(Those who have pointed out that science has never acknowledged cellulite as a special fat puckishly suggest that it was created to "sell you lite" [cellulite] beer and other such products. Actually, according to a 1983 study sponsored by the U.S. Food and Drug Administration, "fat is fat, and cellulite itself is a myth," and the word is of interest chiefly to hucksters selling various products "guaranteed" to get rid of the stuff. Science writer June Roth of the St. Petersburg Times *[Florida], on March 31, 1983, reported on a study, conducted at Johns Hopkins University in Baltimore: "Needle biopsies were taken from people who had lumpy fatty tissue resembling what is being promoted as cellulite. Similar biopsies were taken from people who did not have lumpy fat storage. Pathologists who compared the samples said that all samples looked like ordinary fat cells, and that there was no difference between them." Ordinary fat can look "lumpy" when fat cells just beneath the surface increase in size. As Miss Roth explained, "When this happens, the strands of fibrous tissues that connect the compartments of fat sometimes lose [their] elasticity and cause a bulging, waffy appearance that promoters are calling cellulite.")*

◆ That fasting will shrink your stomach.

(Fasting will not shrink your stomach any more than it will shrink your mouth.)

◆ That if you take a large enough dose of poison, it will not kill you. Similarly, if you take a tiny, tiny dose of poison every day, you will gradually build up an immunity to that poison.

◆ That anyone who has lived to be over 100 has used whiskey, tobacco, or both, for most of his or her life.

HISTORY

- That when you visit the bedroom of an historic home you can show how observant you are by commenting that people used to be much shorter.

  (The preliminary results of a seven-university study of such things indicates that early Americans were not significantly shorter than they are today. The average man in the time of the Revolutionary War was only an inch shorter than today's average.)

- That we are living in a relatively dull period that lacks the vigor and innovation of other times.

  (This credo has apparently been common to many periods. In Stephen Fovargue's A New Catalogue of Vulgar Errors *published in 1767, we are told that a common fallacy of the time was the belief that that period was duller and less ingenious than those past.)*

- That all the great American fortunes were amassed originally by robber barons, economic buccaneers, or wandering old drunks who happened to get lucky at the right time.

- That under the terms of its original admission to the Union, Texas can divide into five separate states, and that if the federal government ever becomes outrageously ornery, ten Texas senators will be in Washington rather than two.

- That history is destined to repeat itself.

- That just west of the Azores in 10,000 feet of water lies the hulk of the German freighter *Deutschland*. It was scuttled there in 1945 with its cargo of $150 million in gold bullion, following the collapse of the Third Reich. This fortune will be used to fund the rise of the Fourth Reich. This could happen any day now.

TIME CAPSULE—1950s COLD WAR INTERLUDE

• That if our army had kept driving across Europe and conquered Russia, we wouldn't have all these postwar problems; that namby-pamby diplomats prevented the military from achieving total victory.

• That although some of Joe McCarthy's tactics were pretty rough, he did a good job in running Commies out of government.

• That if we had threatened to use the A-bomb on Joe Stalin if he didn't behave, he would have become a decent world citizen instantly.

• That the Truman Administration "lost China" through the same bungling that prevented total victory in the war.

◆ That most of the scholars in the time of Columbus thought the earth was flat.

(They didn't.)

◆ That quadruple amputees were sent home during World War II without giving their families warning of their condition. Commonly a man's wife or mother would arrive at the town railroad station to find her "wounded" GI in a basket.

(This belief, which lives on to this day, was extremely common during the war and the decade following. Actually, there were only two individuals who lost all four limbs during the war. Both of these men were greeted as heroes by both the government and the public, which lavished gifts upon them.)

◆ That the Hope diamond and the mummy of King Tut have eternal curses attached to them.

◆ That the stock market crash and ensuing Depression caused the suicide rate to rise alarmingly. That great numbers of able-bodied men spent the period selling apples on street corners.

(There were, of course, suicides and apple sellers, but nothing approximating what has been built up in the popular imagination. Apple

sellers were a convenient subject for photographers who needed a human picture of what was initially an economic event.)

♦ That the bodies of six workers are encased in the concrete of Boulder Dam.

♦ That the abdication speech made over the radio by King Edward VII has been censored. One sentence has been removed from all copies of the recording. If necessary, the British police have entered private homes to remove copies of the speech.

♦ That Mussolini made the trains run on time.

(In their book The Prevalence of Nonsense, *Ashley Montagu and Edward Darling said of this credo, "There was little or no truth in it; people who lived in Italy between the March on Rome [October 28, 1922] and the execution at Como [1945] will bear testimony to the fact that Italian railroads remained as insouciant as ever with regard to timetables and actual schedules. It made no difference to the myth; it never makes any difference. . . .")*

THE KING AND THE STAR OF DAVID—A MYTH EXAMINED

(A report from Bob Skole, who translated and interpreted.)

Bengt Af Klintberg, Swedish sociologist and folklore specialist, in his book *The Rat in the Pizza*, a collection of 100 myths, has one titled "When King Christian Wore the Star of David." The story is that when the Germans ordered Jews in Denmark to wear a yellow six-pointed star, King Christian X refused, saying all Danes are equal. On his morning horseback ride through Copenhagen on the day when the star order was supposed to go into effect, the King wore a yellow six-pointed-star armband. Almost all people in Copenhagen wore such stars, and the Germans rescinded the order.

Af Klintberg writes that a Danish-born American folklorist, Jens Lund, investigated this story, widely told by Jews and Danes in the United States. But unfortunately, Lund found the story not true. The Danish Government opposed Germany's demands for special rules and laws about Jews in 1941, warning there would be demonstrations and sabotage. So the Germans never enforced Jewish discriminatory laws in Denmark. Af Klintberg says that the star incident was linked to King Christian because he symbolized resistance to Hitler. (Almost all of Denmark's Jews escaped to Sweden in 1943, when the Germans finally ordered them rounded up.)

The story originated in 1941 and was widely spread in the United States by Jewish Danes, such as Victor Borge, and was repeated in Leon Uris's *Exodus*. Jens Lund is quoted as saying that its popularity among American Jews is due to the fact that it is one of the few positive stories from a horrible time. "It is based on the hopeful dream of good conquering evil."

◆ That a number of American doughboys and GIs returned home after two World Wars because the bullets that hit them were deflected by Bibles or prayer books that they carried in their breast pockets.

◆ That up to and well into the 1970s aging Japanese soldiers would regularly emerge from the jungles of the South Pacific to finally surrender. In all probability there are still a few of these World War II stragglers at large.

(Yellowed newsclippings prove that there were some stragglers who held on for quite a while after the war was over, but popular mythology turned a few holdouts into legions.)

◆ That nobody still knows what really caused the American Civil War or the Depression.

◆ That the Great Depression was totally caused by unrestricted capitalism.

◆ That no matter what year it happens to be, it is the general consensus that fifteen years earlier: (1) great antiques were cheap and plentiful, (2) food tasted better, (3) there were more fish, (4) things were not as complicated, and (5) people were generally happier.

◆ That in 1626 Peter Minuit bought Manhattan Island for $24 worth of beads and trinkets.

(There seems to have been some sort of an agreement, but an article in the August 9, 1987, Albany Times Union *by Craig*

Brandon had this to say about the bead story: "That's the story, more or less, as it has been handed down to us by history—one of those little anecdotal tidbits accepted without question. Now, along comes Peter Francis Jr., a historian, archaeologist and director of the Center for Bead Research in Lake Placid." He has discovered that the whole story concerning beads and the odd figure of $24 was unmitigated bunkum—a myth without a shred of documentation to back it up. His research, published in the journal New York History, *won the $1,000 Kerr History Prize from the New York State Historical Association for the best article published in 1986.)*

◆ That they don't make 'em (cars, ice-cream cones, ball players, politicians, soldiers, bicycles, pocket combs, typewriters, philosophers, portable radios, grandmothers, books, hamburgers, manservants, family doctors, and a lot of other stuff) like they used to.

◆ That television shows were better twenty years ago, and that the radio shows twenty years before were even better.

◆ That during the period in which American hostages were held in Iran, Iranian students in the United States were able to stay out of harm's way by wearing yarmulkes.

◆ That Sweeney Todd ("the demon barber of Fleet Street") was a real person who once sold meat pies made of human flesh.

◆ That there were widespread premonitions of the fate of *The Titanic,* causing untold hundreds to cancel their reservations on the ill-fated ship.

◆ That large numbers of Vietnam vets are walking time bombs who will explode when given the right stimulus.

(All wars produce psychological victims, and Vietnam was no exception, but somewhere along the line this insidious preconception took hold. Television melodramas featuring exploding Vietnam vets have fed the myth.)

FALKLANDS INTERLUDE

Our prime collector overseas, Bob Skole, has prepared a short account of the classic war myths that sprang up in Sweden at the end of a conflict a decade ago:

"After the Falklands war, the Colombia author and a 1982 Nobel prize winner Gabriel Garcia Marquez wrote a report on the war for a Mexican newspaper. It was translated and published a month or so later by Dagens Nyheter, Sweden's largest morning daily. That story contained, as 'facts,' a number of what I recognize as classic 'war myths.' One, which probably goes back to the Punic Wars, was how an Argentinean soldier back from the Falklands phoned his parents and asked if he could bring home a comrade. Certainly, they said. However, he said he had to warn them that the comrade had lost his legs. The parents said the guy was not welcome, it would be too sad for them to bear. The soldier hung up, and then shot himself, since he was the guy who had lost the legs. (I think I heard that story as a kid about a World War I vet.)

"Another 'fact' by Marquez was how Argentinean soldiers, poorly dressed, had their behinds frozen to the ground as they sat in trenches. Also, how the British Ghurka soldiers, as is their custom, cut ears off Argentineans. The British soldiers (you know their customs!) raped Argentineans they captured."

THE HUMAN CONDITION

◆ That humans are the only species capable of cannibalism.
◆ That the human race is the only species that is sexually active all year long.
◆ That the human race is the only species that kills its own kind.

(This credo is usually hauled out in wartime to underscore the

horrors of human nature. There are many examples, including the lemming, which has been described as the serial killer of the animal world.)

◆ That an intense stare at the back of another can make that person turn around.

◆ That there is no human custom—no matter how disgusting, unnatural, or immoral—that anthropologists have not found to be the norm among the members of remote tribes.

◆ That the "average man" drives a cab, which therefore means that particular notice should be taken of the opinions of cabbies.

◆ That the heart is the seat of the mind.

◆ That merit is always rewarded.

◆ That you get what you pay for.

(You are on an airplane in a seat that cost you $450 and the person sitting next to you is riding in a seat that cost $99 through some super-saver plan. Do you even get an extra bag of nuts?)

◆ That all major disasters come in threes.

◆ That it's unlucky to be superstitious.

◆ That next year's model will be better.

◆ That popular notions can be believed because they represent the accumulated wisdom of the people, and that if they were totally or substantially incorrect we would have stopped repeating them long ago.

(This may be regarded as the keystone credo and may in fact be the most wrongheaded of them all. Few have so successfully stated the case as Albert E. Wiggam in his myth-baiting classic The Marks of a Clear Mind: *"Popular notions are always wrong," he wrote, adding, "the so-called 'accumulated wisdom of the ages' . . . is mostly accumulated tommy-rot.")*

◆ That it is the exception that proves the rule.

(Logic dictates that the exception disprove the rule. A letter from M. B. Helms suggests that an error could have been at work here: It was "The exception probes the rule," originally [and perfectly logical], but the copier from olde English script writing erroneously changed the "b" to "v," which has stayed wrongly with us down through the ages.)

◆ That it is virtually impossible for a person to change.

◆ That practice makes perfect.

(Practice can make perfect, but it often has the effect of compound-

ing error, driving out spontaneity, or simply making things slightly better. A bad actor or high jumper cannot practice his way to perfection. Work for the next decade or two on a really bad golf swing and report back to the authors of this book.)

◆ That you can be down but not out.
◆ That you can make it happen.
◆ That one must pay one's dues, whatever that means.
◆ That nothing is ever as much fun as you remember it being.
◆ That you can run but you can't hide.
◆ That time flies when you're having fun.
◆ That it is not what you know but who you know. (Or, as Joan Rivers said in her commencement address at her daughter's college graduation: "It's not who you know; it's whom you know.")
◆ That good will eventually win out.
◆ That what you see is what you get.
◆ That a rising tide lifts all boats.
◆ That money can't buy happiness.
◆ That beginners are blessed with good luck.
◆ That you can't beat the odds.
◆ That to be a genius is to lack common sense.
◆ That there are certain questions that can never be satisfactorily answered; for example, "What came first, the chicken or the egg?" or "If a tree falls in the forest when no person or animal is near, does it actually make a noise?"
◆ That Mondays are blue.
(Not so, according to researchers reporting in the December 1982 Psychology Today, *which found that it was about the same as other weekdays in terms of mood. Saturdays and Sundays were slightly better.)*
◆ That the crossing of letters in the mail is evidence of something more than mere coincidence.
◆ That no one sleeps well the first time he lies down in a new bed.
◆ That virtue will be rewarded and evil will be punished.
◆ That even though the United Nations is ineffective, it is the best hope we have.

"I" WITNESSES

Some clichéd thoughts take the form of individual declarations that are heard so often that they sound as though they are sung by a chorus—"I hate cats but I love kittens," for instance, or "I can still get [*exaggerated number*] miles to the gallon in my old car." Technically, these declarations are not credos, but they are from the same family.

◆ That I was thinking about you just before you called. (Variation: That I was thinking about you just before your letter arrived.)

◆ That I can get to my office in a flat twenty minutes.

◆ That I never watch television except for documentaries and sports.

◆ That I am not superstitious but I don't take unreasonable chances, either, so I don't walk under ladders, will not accept two-dollar bills, avoid the thirteenth floor of buildings (especially on Friday the thirteenth), and never, never count the number of cars in a funeral procession.

◆ That it isn't the money, it's the principle of the thing.

◆ That large numbers of checks are in the mail.

(This, of course, comes from the oft-heard declaration that the check is in the mail. Another credo to go with it: "That millions of postcards are lost annually." When people come back from vacation, they often say, "Didn't you get the postcard I sent you? It's amazing how bad the mail has gotten.")

◆ That I'm not revengeful but I'll get you for that.

◆ That if it weren't for the children, we'd live in the city.

◆ That there is something intrinsically wrong with public-opinion polls because neither I nor anybody I know has ever been contacted for one.

◆ That I have a sense of humor.

(No American, no matter how sullen, will admit to not having a sense of humor.)

◆ That I usually break even when I go to Las Vegas.

◆ I know it looks like I've been overeating. The truth is that it is my metabolism—that is, my body retains a lot of water. And I haven't ruled out the possibility that it's glandular.

◆ That flea markets are generally dreadful affairs, but I have made some stunning finds at them.

(If all the tales of great flea-market finds were true, there would be no need for a Social Security system, since we would all have a closet full of Paul Revere silver, Stradivarius violins, and the like to sell during our old age.)

◆ That Polish jokes are rude and demeaning to a proud nationality, but while I'm thinking about it, have you heard about the Pole who . . .

JOURNALISM

◆ That if at some odd hour of the night you are determined to know the name of the last left-handed National League pitcher to hit a triple with two on in the World Series, you can call the city desk of any large newspaper and someone will know the answer.

◆ That writing for a newspaper so dulls one's talent that no readable literature has ever been produced by a former journalist.

◆ That writing for a newspaper teaches one the discipline necessary to produce readable literature.

◆ That writing for a newspaper is irrelevant to one's literary future.

◆ That journalists are irresponsible whelps who do not have to suffer the consequences of their actions; nonetheless, freedom of the press must be preserved lest the Republic collapse.

◆ That newspaper columnists are able to spit out 750 words

of compelling prose in twenty minutes flat with all sorts of noise and commotion going on around them.

◆ That you should never buy the newspaper on the top of the pile.

◆ That blown-dry anchormen on local television news shows get to know the "pulse of the people" by appearing at shopping-center promotional events, an activity far more valuable, journalistically, than actually reporting a story from time to time.

◆ That the New York-Washington–based liberal media haven't the foggiest notion of what is going on in the rest of the country.

◆ That they wouldn't print it if it wasn't true.

◆ That newspapermen are hard-bitten and cynical, and know far more than they dare put into print.

◆ That the six and eleven o'clock newscasts cover all the news worth reporting that day (save those nights "Nightline" stays on for more than half an hour due to the crucial nature of its subject matter: i.e., male infertility).

◆ That in order for something to appear in *Reader's Digest* it must have appeared somewhere else before; in fact, the *Digest* will plant an article in a minor magazine if it wants to publish that article.

LAW

◆ That whenever a contested will goes to court, the lawyers wind up with most of the money, while the deserving heirs receive little or nothing; this is especially true when the deceased did not have the foresight to leave a written testament.

◆ That there is such a thing as international law, which, for instance, requires the citizen of one nation to help the citizen of another if that person is floundering in international waters.

◆ That lawyers employ secret techniques to select jurors apt to be friendly to their causes, to wit:

-Jews and Italians are warmhearted, while Irishmen and some Scandinavians are thought to be colder.
-Women jurors resent attractive women plaintiffs or defendants.
-Former accident victims rarely award another plaintiff more than they received in their own case.
-People in the arts are tolerant, whereas bankers and farmers tend to be conservative.

◆ That laughing juries never convict.
◆ That anybody who can read English and follow forms available at any public law library can represent himself in a simple lawsuit.
◆ That you can go out and make a "citizen's arrest." This can be done in virtually all circumstances, even when a policeman is caught breaking the law.
(Ask anyone in law enforcement; the concept of a citizen's arrest is pure fiction.)
◆ That possession is nine-tenths of the law.
◆ That you can shoot an intruder, trespasser, or adulterer and expect only a slap on the wrist. If you do it in Texas you can forget the slap on the wrist.
◆ That lawyers in divorce cases fuel any hostility between the mates to increase the time of settlement, which means higher fees.
◆ That the most bloodthirsty crimes are often effectively pardoned because minute procedural errors—having nothing to do with guilt or innocence—have been made handling the guilty party.
(It has happened, but the hand-wringers make it sound like an everyday affair.)
◆ That you can legally accuse anyone of anything if you make sure to use the word "alleged."
◆ That a written contract is absolutely binding and that one who has signed a contract may be forced to do something that he now does not wish to do.

◆ That the judicial establishment protects its own, which is why the nation must put up with a number of absolutely loony judges.

(Judges are subject to judicial scrutiny just like other members of the legal establishment.)

◆ That the lawyer who argues the loudest will lose the case because he has decibels, not the law, on his side. (This law is invalid in county seats with populations of less than 7,500, and in the courts of Philadelphia, Pennsylvania.)

◆ That if a witness coughs on the stand or shifts his eyes around the courtroom, he's lying.

◆ That you can go out and commit murder and the lawyer can get you free . . . as long as you've got the money.

◆ That a shyster is the lawyer representing the party on the other side of your lawsuit.

LITERATURE

◆ That everyone has a life story that would make a good book. All that is needed is for someone to sit down with him and help put it on paper. The movie and paperback money will be divided equally.

◆ That an author is flattered when you ask to borrow a copy of his book, for it shows you are not a conventional reader who is content to settle for just any copy the book dealer might have on the shelf.

◆ That an author is further flattered when you state that you are waiting to buy his book in paperback, because you are affirming your faith in his commercial appeal and money-earning potential.

◆ That an author is flattered when you say you checked out his latest book from the library, because your interest means his library sales should jump immeasurably.

◆ That getting a book published makes you rich and famous

and that if that book is optioned or considered for a movie, the author becomes fabulously wealthy.

◆ That if you put enough monkeys in front of enough typewriters, it would just be a matter of time before one of them typed *King Lear* or the entire works of Shakespeare (or the Bible, or whatever piece of literature you favor).

◆ That Jules Verne and H. G. Wells predicted virtually all of the inventions and technical trends of the modern era.

◆ That E. L. Doctorow is a pseudonym for another writer or group of writers.

(Among other versions, it was reported in The New York Times Book Review *of February 7, 1982, by Edwin McDowell, that there were two Doctorow rumors then active in the Southwest: "The first was that the author of* Ragtime *is actually a committee of 'eight ladies,' hence the initials E. L. The other was that the author is a reclusive black doctor whose initials are O. W.; that is, Doctor O. W., or Doctorow.")*

◆ That most bartenders and cabbies could write great books, but never do.

◆ That if an author goes into a store and autographs his or her own book, it is as good as sold because the store cannot send it back to the publisher for credit.

◆ That writers smoke pipes, wear tweed jackets, and work four and a half hours a day.

◆ That many of the female authors of gothic novels are in fact portly, bald, cigar-chomping men.

(Reacting to this credo, the editor of the earlier incarnation of this book, Sandi Gelles-Cole, wrote the authors: "Trust me, many of the female authors of gothic novels are, indeed, rather portly, bald, cigar-chomping men.")

◆ That there are only [fill in with any number from three to fifteen] basic themes in literature and that every novel and short story you will ever see is a variation on one of the basic themes.

◆ That you can't judge a book by its cover.

Love, Marriage, and Sex

~~~~~~~

♦ That sexual mores are not that much different from the way they were thirty years ago, the main difference being that people talk more about it today.

♦ That a twenty-three-year-old male is really convincing someone other than himself when he avows he purchases *Playboy* and *Penthouse* magazines for their articles, rather than other features printed as centerfolds in living flesh colors.

♦ That there is love at first sight, that opposites attract, and that absence makes the heart grow fonder.

♦ That if it had not been for *National Geographic,* vast numbers of now middle-aged American men would not have known that puberty had begun.

♦ That June is the luckiest month to get married in.

♦ That no one who is married is really happy.

♦ That no one who is single is really happy.

♦ That all people who are not married would like to be; that all unmarried women are looking for a mate; that it is always better for a woman to stay home with her children than to go to work; that it is always a tragedy when a couple divorces; if they have children, it is even worse.

♦ That a wife never feels truly comfortable with her husband's friends from his bachelor days.

♦ That southern women are more beautiful than northern women.

♦ That buxom ladies are less intelligent than those who aren't.

♦ That women can withstand colder temperatures because of additional "fatty tissue."

◆   That bras were burned during the early days of the modern women's movement.

(Quoting Ellen Goodman: "Someday when they write a media history of the women's movement, the chapter on the 1970s will be called 'The Bra-Burning That Never Happened.' This will focus on the nationwide report of the Flaming Feminists who set a torch to their underwear. In fact, no piece of lingerie was ever kindled in anger, but from then on, women's rights advocates were permanently labeled 'bra-burners.' " Ms. Goodman to the contrary, one of the authors witnessed, in a reportorial capacity, a conflagration fueled by bras at a demonstration on the Atlantic City boardwalk outside the Democratic National Convention in August 1964.)

◆   That any lie on a marriage license makes it null and void.

(A falsehood between consenting adults does not automatically void such an agreement.)

◆   That a symptom of pregnancy is a craving for ice cream and pickles.

◆   That women in primitive cultures have a much easier time in childbirth than women in more developed cultures.

◆   That men have one less rib than women.

◆   That when a young and proper woman goes out to dinner with a man, she should avoid restaurants where there are white tablecloths as these will remind him of sheets and stir his lust.

(Told to a woman by a nun in a Catholic high school.)

◆   That lesbians always wear short hair.

◆   That most teenagers—particularly *your* teenagers—have only a vague notion of what sex is, and no inclination to try it unless they've had a sex-education class.

◆   That in women sexual enjoyment is directly correlated with education; hence the more educated a woman, the more frequently she experiences orgasm. Uneducated women, conversely, never enjoy orgasm.

(Sociologist Lynn Eden, responsible for this credo, says persons in her profession call this a "spurious variable," i.e., bunk.)

◆   That unusually high numbers of children are born at the time of the full moon.

(Despite studies to the contrary, this belief is still widely held, especially among nurses, who should know better. For reasons unclear,

professionals often err on the side of mythology, e.g., police officers who insist that the worst human behavior is displayed under a full moon.)

◆ That an abnormally high number of babies are born nine months from the time of a power outage, blackout, or evening when normal TV programing is preempted by news.

(In More Misinformation, *Tom Burnam reports that a study of the effects of the New York blackout of 1965 showed a slight decrease.)*

◆ That it's unlucky to give away a wedding present.

◆ That women who ride horses are oversexed.

◆ That a small but nonetheless significant percentage of the people who are walking the streets are there because of drugstore clerks who, with pins, poked holes in condom packages.

◆ That people with particularly active sex lives tend to have extra energy to apply to other pursuits.

◆ That people whose sex lives are inactive tend to have extra energy to apply to other pursuits.

◆ That you can tell if a person is a virgin by the way they walk.

◆ That homosexuals are uniformly creative and graceful and are hardly ever dullards.

◆ That heterosexual males are generally clumsy.

◆ That extremely handsome men tend to be gay.

◆ That there are very few blue-collar homosexuals.

◆ That you can always tell a gay male by the way he dresses; that gay men are more fashionable; that gay men love clothes in order to compensate for unhappy lives; that gay clones are as conformist (macho, antirevolutionary, woman-hating) as their clothing.

(Jeff Weinstein, who wrote about gay affairs for The Village Voice, *cites these "credos" under what he regards as their more proper designation—he calls them "four lies about gay male fashion.")*

MILITARY

◆ That the Air Force could teach apes to fly but couldn't make them salute.

◆ That the Navy has a ten-day supply of any necessary item, such as fuel or ordnance, and a fifty-year supply of oyster forks for the officers' mess.

◆ That the armed forces of the United States have and will always make colossal mistakes in assignments—for example, assigning trombonists to tank repair and putting mechanics in the Army band.

◆ That the Pentagon has spent billions of taxpayer dollars on mindless research projects having to do with the dynamics of yo-yos, the masturbatory habits of elk, and the use of agricultural metaphor in Icelandic folklore.

◆ That there are no atheists in foxholes.

◆ That whoever controls the Indian Ocean controls the world.

◆ That recyclers turned surplus World War II naval vessels into razor blades.

◆ That the brass at the Pentagon routinely substitute sea gull for chicken in mess halls.

◆ That there is a hidden ward of World War I, World War II, Korean War, and Vietnam War veterans at Walter Reed that is so gruesome that nurses who are assigned there go crazy after a year and have to be treated at a special hospital out West.

This is adjacent to the 450-bed facility that the Catholic Church maintains to dry out alcoholic priests. Just over the hill is the CIA's "sex camp," where vacationing covert agents can enjoy feminine companionship without fear of compromise.

Four thousand miles to the west is the island where the Marine Corps permanently quarantined the hardened killers it did not dare return to the United States after the Second

World War. They have Polynesian wives and unlimited supplies of Schlitz Beer.

◆ That because there were on occasion references to death and devastation, "M★A★S★H" gives us a pretty good idea of what the Korean War was really like, and that for the same reason "China Beach" accurately reflected the horrors of the Vietnam War.

◆ That the body of an enemy soldier was found chained to his machine gun. (Sometimes it's a tank crewman chained in his tank.)

◆ That there is a particularly fierce and bloodthirsty enemy unit commanded by a woman. In a common variation, the woman is described as having only one breast.

◆ That people in the military don't mind being uprooted every few years, severing friendships, because they secretly enjoy it and get such good deals at the PX and commissary.

◆ That every successful military unit has an innovative supply sergeant who can start out with a dented canteen and trade his way upward to two carloads of steaks and a tanker of beer.

◆ That the Pentagon was originally designed as a military hospital to take care of the casualties from the projected invasion of the Japanese islands.

(This has shown up in a number of places, including the novel Brimstone, *by Robert L. Duncan, from which this credo is quoted. The truth is that it was built early in World War II to consolidate the then War Department's scattered offices around Washington.)*

◆ That the Air Force has discovered the true nature of UFOs but is keeping it secret in the interest of national security.

(The U.S. Air Force is so deluged with queries about UFOs that in January 1985 it issued a "fact sheet" summarizing research through "Project Blue Book," which started in 1969. ["Blue Book" was headquartered at Wright-Patterson Air Force Base in Ohio, which as any space theorist knows is the same place where frozen bodies of "Little Green Men from Space" are stored in a refrigerated vault.] According to the sheet: "From 1947 to 1969, a total of 12,618 sightings were reported to Project Blue Book. Of these, 701 remained 'unidentified.' " The study concluded: "(1) no UFO reported, investigated, and evaluated by the Air Force has ever given any indication of threat to our national security; (2) there has been no ev-

idence submitted to or discovered by the Air Force that sightings categorized as 'unidentified' represent technological developments or principles beyond the range of present-day scientific knowledge; and (3) there has been no evidence indicating that sightings categorized as 'unidentified' are extraterrestrial vehicles."

Project Blue Book records are now stored in the Modern Military Branch of the National Archives in Washington, D.C.—thirty-seven cubic feet of files on individual sightings, three cubic feet of files relating to their investigation, and two cubic feet of administrative files. A cubic foot comprises about 2,000 pages. The records are also on ninety-four rolls of microfilm.

The fact sheet disposes of the "Little Green Men" thusly: "Periodically, it is erroneously stated that the remains of extraterrestrial visitors are or have been stored at Wright-Patterson AFB. There are not now, nor ever have been, any extraterrestrial visitors or equipment at Wright-Patterson Air Force Base."

In 1992 rumors of a supersecret superplane capable of flying at eight times the speed of sound were dignified by stories in the respected publications Jane's Defense Weekly, a British journal, and Aviation Week & Space Technology. In turn, The Washington Post and The New York Times ran front-page stories discussing supposedly authoritative sightings of large and unusually shaped planes leaving peculiar condensation trails at high altitude—"Donuts on a rope," according to a description offered by John Mintz of The Washington Post on December 14, 1992. Unexplained rumbling sounds and booms were also heard from Edwards Air Force Base in the California desert, where odd military planes are often tested, and at Nellis Air Force Base, a remote facility in Nevada that is off-limits to most of humanity. The mystery was enhanced by the appearance of a $2 billion budget item in the Defense Department budget in 1985 referring to "Aurora." No further unclassified explanation was offered.

Writers such as William Sweetman of Jane's Defense Weekly theorized that "Aurora" was a code name for a new spy plane that would succeed the Lockheed SR-71 "Blackbird," which retired in 1990 after a quarter century of surveillance service. But all hands denied that any such craft existed—including Secretary of the Air Force Donald Rice, who said that the reports were "fantasy" and added that since his service would operate such planes if they existed, he certainly would know about them.

The New York Times *finally chose sides in an article on January 18, 1993, by science writer Malcolm W. Browne, summarized by the headline* RUMORS OF U.S. SUPERPLANE APPEAR UNFOUNDED. *Ironically, Browne said, the Russians seemed further along on developing a superspeed spy plane than the United States. The Federation of American Scientists, which is cool toward military spending, and especially that involving intelligence gathering, agreed. Its director, Dr. John E. Pike, theorized why the "Aurora" reports gained such credence even among serious military and space writers. Pike wrote in the federation's newsletter in December 1992: "Belief in the existence of marvelously capable and highly secret aircraft resonates with some of the deeper anxieties of contemporary American society . . . The declining fortunes of the American aerospace industry have created growing uncertainties about the future. It would be comforting to believe that the decline of America and American airspace was more apparent than real."*

Now, if the Air Force would only explain that undulating blue light that we saw over the Washington area last evening . . .)

Misnomers and Mistaken Identities

One of our faithful helpmates and credo collectors, Bill Gerk of Burlingame, California, has correctly pointed out that a book of this scope needs a list of common misnomers. He has offered up some of his favorites, to which we have added some of our own.

◆ That a Jerusalem artichoke is not an artichoke, it's a sunflower.

◆ That a ten-gallon hat does not hold 10 gallons—closer to 1 gallon.

◆ That hedgehogs and groundhogs are not hogs.

◆ That a quahog is not a hog but an edible clam.

◆ That a beeline and as the crow flies are not straight lines—bees and crows zigzag all over the place.

◆ That the cucumber is not a vegetable; botanically, it's a fruit. So are the eggplant, pumpkin, squash, tomato, gherkin, and okra.

◆ That a rhubarb is not a fruit; botanically, it's a vegetable.

◆ That a polecat is not a cat. It's a skunk.

◆ That Greenland was so misnamed to encourage others to settle there. Iceland should be called Greenland.

◆ That a tea kettle is not a tea kettle. It's a water kettle.

◆ That a Komodo dragon is not a dragon. It's a lizard.

◆ That Rocky Mountain oysters are not oysters. They are testicles.

◆ That Welsh rabbit is not a rabbit. It is melted cheese mixed with ale or beer served on crackers or toast.

◆ That marsh rabbits sold in stores are not rabbits. They are muskrats.

◆ That tube steak is not steak. It's a humorous name for a hot dog.

◆ That Salisbury steak is not steak. It's a fancy name for hamburger.

◆ That a tin can is not mainly tin. It is 98 to 99-1/2 percent steel and only thinly coated with tin.

◆ That the Cape of Good Hope was originally called the Cape of Storms.

◆ That a leechee nut is not a nut. It's a dried fruit.

◆ That a musk ox is not an ox. It's a sheep.

◆ That Lincoln was wrong in his Gettysburg speech. Lincoln said, "The world will little note nor long remember what we say here. . . ."

◆ That involuntary servitude is not allowed in the United States. Our Constitution permits it as punishment for crime.

◆ That heartburn comes from the heart. Heartburn is a backflow of acid stomach contents into the throat.

◆ That the pigskin on the football field is anything other than cowhide.

◆ That the Canary Islands are named for canaries. They are named after a breed of dogs.

◆ That the horseshoe crab is not a crab. It's an arachnid—not a crustacean.

◆ That a black-eyed pea (cowpea) is not a pea but a bean (legume).

◆ That the term "football" does not derive from the kicking of a ball. Rather it originated after rugby players started throwing the ball.

◆ That water on the knee is not water. It is synovial fluid—a thick, colorless lubricating fluid that acts as a shock absorber.

◆ That corn does not mean corn in England, Ireland, or Scotland. Corn means wheat in England. Corn means oats in Ireland or Scotland.

◆ That there are no buffalo in the United States. Technically, they are bison.

◆ That Brazil nuts are exported mainly from Brazil but are grown chiefly in Bolivia.

◆ That vodka did not start in Russia. Rather it appeared in Poland as far back as the 1070s.

◆ That the glass snake is not a snake nor is it made of glass. It's a lizard. It has eyelids and solid jawbones.

◆ That Irish stew is not Irish but German.

◆ That the Irish in Ireland seldom eat corned beef and cabbage.

◆ That most chamois are from a rare goatlike antelope. Most today come from deer, goats, and sheep.

◆ That the Pennsylvania Dutch are not Dutch. They are German.

◆ That the wise old owl isn't. Owls have low IQs.

◆ That hay fever is usually not caused by hay nor is it a fever. Hay fever is called that because it happens during haying season. Usually the allergies derive from pollen and ragweed.

◆ That a jellyfish is not a fish. It is a coelenterate.

◆ That raspberries and strawberries are botanically not berries. They belong to the rose family.

◆ That poison ivy is not an ivy, nor is poison oak an oak. Each is a member of the sumac family.

◆ That the cashew nut is a member of the poison ivy family.

◆ That kilts are not native to Scotland. They were brought into Scotland by a French tailor in 1745.

◆ That bagpipes did not originate in Scotland. Similar instruments were used in Chaldea, Egypt, Greece, and Persia. The Romans introduced bagpipes to the British Isles.

◆ That English walnuts did not originate in England. They are native to Persia.

◆ That the glove compartment in a car isn't used for gloves. Polls show that the percentage of people who keep gloves in their glove compartments is close to zero.

◆ That glass is not a solid. Technically, glass is a liquid because it is cooled rapidly to prevent crystallization.

NATIONALITIES

◆ That if a foreigner in America cannot speak English, he lacks a certain amount of intelligence. However, the reverse is not true of an American abroad.

◆ That Americans have the highest standard of living in the world.

(Measuring the "highest" or "best" standard of living is a highly subjective undertaking; one of the authors insists that statistical evidence notwithstanding, the Shenandoah Valley of Virginia offers more amenities than any locale on earth.)

◆ That it is always a shame when the third generation of American-born descendants of someone from the Old Country speaks only English, knows no ethnic dances, and would rather go to Disney World than to the Old Country to visit distant cousins who speak no English and live in grubby little towns with no indoor toilets.

◆ That something insidious is tearing at the fabric of American life, which is made evident by the contract demands of professional athletes and the behavior of rock stars.

◆ That the average American is a wellspring of common sense and is never hoodwinked for long.

◆ That any American believes he can perform three tasks better than the people who are currently doing them: teach school, govern the state, and edit the local newspaper.

◆ That if a person doesn't speak very good English, you must shout at him to be understood.

◆ That millions of people in this world dream of having their picture taken by an American tourist.

◆ That the English Channel is all that keeps Great Britain from being overrun by packs of rabid dogs from the Continent, and that once the "chunnel" connecting France and Britain is finished, the country will be inundated with mad dogs.

(Correspondent Joseph Lelyveld wrote in The New York Times *on December 26, 1985, that this is a "deep-seated British folk belief," and that 88 percent of Englishmen polled felt that "rabies would be greatly increased or virtually unstoppable" if the tunnel was built. Then Prime Minister Margaret Thatcher went ahead with chunnel plans anyway, apparently satisfied that whatever its other flaws, France is not overpopulated with rabid mutts.)*

◆ That most French-Canadian women are named Marie.

◆ That most Mexican women are named Maria.

◆ That the average European has better taste than the average American.

◆ That English lords are wastrels and drink too much port; when they open their estates to the public for fee tours, however, they can be charming and out-of-the-mold.

◆ That French is a pretty language and German an ugly one.

◆ That despite their many graces, the French are incredibly rude to Americans, especially if they are trying to speak French with less than perfect fluency.

◆ That the only watch worth owning comes from Switzerland.

◆ That the average Swiss is trilingual, thrifty, and politically neutral.

- That the Danes and Norwegians have never forgiven the Swedes for their neutrality during World War II.
- That Swedes are sullen, sexually promiscuous, and suicidal.
- That the Irish say "Begorra," Swedes "Yumpin' Yiminey," French *"Sacrebleu,"* Germans *"Was ist das?",* et cetera, whenever they have nothing better to say.
- That the Russians are an artless, clumsy crew except when it comes to the ballet.
- That the Irish are drunkards.
- That Asians are notoriously bad drivers.
- That a Russian would gladly hand over six months' wages and his firstborn child for a pair of Levi's jeans, a carton of Kents, and a UCLA sweatshirt.
- That despite their fits of indignation when they hear Polish jokes, Poles secretly enjoy the attention.
- That Chinese inscrutability is a constant.
- That the Vatican has huge (but unspecified) commercial holdings in the United States.
- That the majority of blind or otherwise handicapped beggars encountered in foreign cities are frauds who make good money through their deception. It is also so that the blind beggar whom you would guess to be a fraud is most likely to be the neediest of all.
- That you can always tell where Scandinavian loggers have worked because the ground is littered with Copenhagen snuff can lids.

PHYSICAL CHARACTERISTICS

- That a soft voice is a sign of good breeding in a man.
- That a firm handshake is a sign of honesty, that a weak

handshake means the person is suspicious and should be watched, that a damp handshake is a sign of nervousness.

♦ That if a short man is aggressive, it's because he is so short; if he is not, it's because he is so short.

♦ That there are some people who cannot wear watches because of some mysterious bodily effect that causes them to stop.

♦ That "spread" is the inevitable consequence of middle age.

(As both authors would concede under cross-examination, blaming "spread" on middle age is a rationalization for not exercising or eating properly.)

♦ That a strong back and weak mind are just as surely paired as a strong mind and a weak back.

♦ That a square jaw is a sign of determination in a person.

♦ That slender hands signify artistic ability, as do long slender fingers.

♦ That bushy eyebrows are a certain sign of sexuality in a male; that long fingers hint at a related development; that a woman who constantly licks her lips is deserving of special attention.

♦ That blondes have more fun, tan better, and are generally dumber.

♦ That brunettes are more trustworthy than blondes.

♦ That redheads have quick and violent tempers.

♦ That a hairy chest is a sign of strength.

♦ That black skin gives greater protection against sunburn and heat prostration.

(In his 1946 book The Natural History of Nonsense, *Bergen Evans eloquently states: ". . . the belief that the Negro is 'equipped' to endure heat better than the white man serves to distract attention from the fact that he is not. Millions of Negroes work long hours in the hot sun for others' profit, and it is easier and cheaper for the others to believe that the Negroes 'just naturally don't mind' than it would be to provide shorter hours, rest periods, and cool drinking water. Yet, contrary to general belief, the pigmentation of their skin affords them no great protection from sunburn or heat prostration." Evans went on to cite life insurance statistics that showed that two to six times as many blacks were dying from heat as whites.)*

♦ That you should not trust anyone with one long eyebrow.

♦ That if you pull a gray hair out of your head, a dozen more will grow in its place.

♦ That if your right ear rings, someone is speaking positively about you. If the left ear rings, someone is speaking negatively about you.

♦ That if your nose itches, you can expect company.

♦ That any male who wears a short haircut works for IBM or the FBI, or is a Marine.

♦ That shifty-eyed people are more likely to be dishonest than those with a fixed gaze.

(From a 1977 Associated Press dispatch: "There is no connection between eye-gaze fixity and honesty. On the contrary, one study showed that, compared with normal persons, psychopathic liars actually maintained steadier eye contact in speaking with others.")

♦ That shaving makes hair grow in faster and thicker.

(The rate of hair growth is predetermined by hereditary factors, and shaving or not shaving will have no effect on the rate of growth. Frank Brusea has written us on this subject: "This sounds stupid, but for an entire summer I shaved so I could grow a beard. It wasn't until the end of the summer that I realized that not *shaving promotes beard growth.")*

♦ That big ears are a sign of generosity, while small ears denote a stingy person. A "big head little wit, little head not a bit." A high brow denotes noble character and a low one stupidity. A man with close-set eyes is mean, while one with a long nose or crossed eyes has a cranky disposition. A long chin signifies jealousy, and large lips indicate a grouch. Buck teeth indicate a tattler. If a man's eyebrows meet, he is sure to have a fiery disposition.

♦ That a wide and bald forehead is a sign of genius.

♦ That too lush a beard or an excess of body hair encourages baldness.

♦ That men with beards are hiding something (or hiding from something).

♦ That you can judge the size of a man's organ by the size of his nose, thumb, or feet.

♦ That fat women always have good skin and pretty faces.

♦ That gap-toothed women are oversexed.

♦ That any person, regardless of prominence or outward

poise, has a secret Achilles' heel that is shielded from the public.

(In truth, some may have two Achilles' heels, others none.)

◆ That the color of a woman's eyebrows match the hue of more private body hair.

POLITICS

◆ That Congress would be so much more effective if it were not for the fact that it is overloaded with lawyers.

◆ That politicians aren't crooked until after their first term in office.

◆ That 500 people pulled off the street at random would run the nation as well as Congress—and get into less trouble.

◆ That an incumbent president is always reelected if the closing Dow-Jones industrial average is higher the Monday before the election than it was on the opening day of the election year.

(If this old axiom were true, Jimmy Carter would have been reelected in 1980—the average on election eve was 937.20, up from 824.57 on the year's first day of trading.

◆ That high-quality American political leadership is a thing of the past.

◆ That politics makes strange bedfellows.

(Upon examination, even the oddest of political alliances usually has an underlying rationale—i.e., bootleggers in the South long made common cause with ministers in support of laws prohibiting liquor sales, the first group motivated by profit, the second by theology.)

◆ That politicians with whom you disagree have sold out to big business, big labor, and/or other special-interest groups, whereas politicians who share your views reached their conclusions by carefully weighing the issues.

◆ That generals make lousy presidents. But in retrospect,

George Washington seemed to have done all right and Eisenhower wasn't all that bad either.

♦ That there are secret basement hideaways in Congressional office buildings in which members indulge in drinking binges and sexual orgies during the lunch hour, which extends from eleven-thirty A.M. until four-thirty P.M., and that Capitol police are chosen on the understanding they look the other way.

♦ That the presidency of the United States is too big a job for one man.

♦ That Hertz, Avis, National, and Budget will not rent cars to Senator Teddy Kennedy.

♦ That if the TV networks kept their cameras on the nonsense of the podium for an entire political convention, viewers would turn to game shows and movie reruns. That by the second night of an uncontested convention, most people do so anyway.

♦ That the war would have been over in six months if we'd elected Goldwater. Or McCarthy. Or Humphrey. Or McGovern. Or Wallace.

♦ That if all the people who say that they did not vote for Nixon actually did not vote for Nixon, he never would have been elected president.

♦ That the president must be a member of a church and attend its public ceremonies regularly.

♦ That regardless of what services he might be performing to better the Republic, a vice-president of the United States must be viewed with the condescension one reserves for an unemployed brother-in-law or the neighborhood crank. That each new president avows his vice-president is to have a significant policy-making role in the administration, a vow that has tended to last as long as three weeks.

♦ That an intelligent politician consults the actuarial tables before accepting the nomination for vice-president.

♦ That Democrats squabble like a roomful of wet cats at their national political conventions, but always manage to unite by November and win (except in those years when they don't and lose).

♦ That the banalities of political convention speeches should be forgiven because no one expects anything else from the party hacks chosen to deliver them.

◆ That Democrats aren't all that bad, once you sit down and have a drink with them.

◆ That Republicans aren't all that bad, once you sit down and have a drink with them.

◆ That Democrats don't really drink more than Republicans. They just seem that way because they were drunker when they started.

◆ That you shouldn't talk politics or religion with strangers at a party.

PROFESSIONALS

◆ That all dentists have hairy arms.

◆ That librarians are dour old ladies with a yellow pencil protruding through their bun hairdos and wearing horn-rimmed glasses.

◆ That preachers' sons never amount to anything and that their daughters are sexually active at age fifteen.

(This has been an American credo for generations. Several major studies have been made to see if there is any truth to this supposition, including one by Havelock Ellis, who concluded that "eminent children of the clergy considerably outnumber those of lawyers, doctors, and army officers put together.")

◆ That barbers and bartenders think they're amateur psychologists and will talk your leg off.

◆ That cabdrivers know secret routes, based mainly upon back alleys and other secondary thoroughfares, that get them across Washington, or midtown New York, twice as fast as you could in your own car; that most drivers are Archie Bunker prototypes, but you listen to them anyway as keen barometers of public opinion, especially on the subjects of office-holders, civil rights, and municipal highway improvement programs.

(Passengers in taxicabs, particularly out-of-town journalists, frequently mistake garrulity for wisdom.)
◆ That there is a taxi driver in Cleveland, or maybe Toledo, who speaks only in response to direct questions. We think.
◆ That higher pay attracts more-qualified people.
(You hear this one a lot from politicians, teachers, and other public employees.)
◆ That truckers always help motorists in distress.
◆ That there are no blond morticians.
◆ That an ability to quote the Scripture enhances a minister's expertise at saving sinners from eternal damnation, and makes him a more credible figure to his lodge brothers.
◆ That admirals flounder in twelve-foot sailboats and astronauts are all thumbs when it comes to piloting light planes.
◆ That being an accountant is a boring job.
◆ That an accountant caters to lazy or stupid people or people who are looking for all the loopholes.
◆ That great mathematicians cannot balance their own checkbooks, stockbrokers tend to bet heavily on horse races, chefs rely on convenience foods at home, and doctors often overlook less-than-major illness and injury in their own homes.
◆ That the life span of an oboe player is five years less than the national average due to the "mysterious" pitch and aural vibrations emitted by the instrument.

FARMERS' CREDOS

• That carrying a buckeye in one's pocket will ward off arthritis and head colds.
• That leaving the carcass of a coyote or a crow on a fence will dissuade the appearance of other predators.
• That thunder will sour fresh milk.
(The sudden temperature changes associated with thunderstorms give this credo a surface credibility.)
• That brokers on the Chicago commodity exchanges make far

more from each year's crops than the farmers who actually grow them.

- That hogs should not be butchered until first frost.

(Again, a credo linked to the weather: cool temperatures mean less chance of meat spoiling during dressing.)

- That leaving a small portion of food on one's plate after each meal ensures that the plate will never be empty during the coming year.

PSYCHOLOGY

◆ That many cases of mental illness could be prevented if people would only take a little time to "get hold of themselves."

◆ That you can't change human nature.

◆ That people who are crazy or off balance become more so when there is a full moon.

(Despite the fact that this has been disproven in studies that look at such things as the relative number of people admitted to mental hospitals during periods when the moon is full, the belief persists.

Perhaps the final word on this bit of nonsense appeared in a summary article on twelve—count 'em, twelve—studies of crisis calls to police stations, crisis-intervention centers, poison-control units, etc., and the phases of the moon, which appeared in a 1992 issue of Psychology Reports. *The review of the dozen studies concluded that there is "no good foundation for the belief that lunar phase is related to the frequency of crisis calls. In addition, there is no evidence whatsoever for the contention that calls of a more emotional or 'out-of-control' nature occur more often at the full moon."*

The notion is probably tied to the ancient belief that insanity was linked to moon [hence, lunatic *for a crazy person] and which has been reinforced in our time by horror films in which the full moon is required before the monster can take center stage.)*

◆   That psychiatrists' children are always in need of a psychiatrist (just as shoemakers' children have holes in their shoes).

◆   That therapists have more problems than their patients, and that female clients are convinced that seduction on the couch is the only route to a swift cure.

(This has, of course, happened, but on nothing approaching the scale it reaches in popular legend.)

◆   That you can be hypnotized against your will.

◆   That bright people are more likely to have nervous breakdowns than dull ones.

◆   That the holiday season brings on depression in large numbers of people.

(A number of major news organizations have attempted to nail this myth. A New York Times *roundup on this subject on Christmas Eve 1983 was entitled "The 'Holiday Blues' Found to Be a Libel on Christmastime." A number of independent researchers have worked to debunk this one, including:*

•   *Ohio State University psychiatrist Stephen Pariser, who has studied the phenomenon of holiday depression and concluded that it is a creation of the media and that there is little evidence to support the contention that depression is any greater in December than in July.*

•   *Drs. James Hillard and John Buckman of the University of Virginia Center, in a study reported in the* Journal of the American Medical Association *in December 1983. In fact, they wrote, the number of suicides, psychiatric hospitalizations, and even letters to advice columns is relatively low in December compared to other months. According to an Associated Press summary dated December 16, 1983, the researchers found that "the season triggers a variety of emotions and conflicts but that few people fail to cope with them.")*

◆   That certain dreams, especially nightmares, foretell disasters.

◆   That many persons come away from their consultations feeling that the psychiatrist is nuttier than they are. He sometimes is.

Regions

♦ That any given New England farmer has more common sense than a Harvard professor. This holds true as well for Texas shrimp fishermen, New York cabdrivers, and bricklayers in Seattle, Washington.

♦ That if you prowl the back roads of rural New England, you will chance across small inns run by hospitable couples who serve four-star meals, provide comfortable featherbed rooms with a fireplace, and send you on the way in the morning with a country breakfast and a smile, for less than twenty dollars. Unfortunately, these places are never pinpointed in guidebooks.

♦ That all small New England towns are in possession of at least one haunted house, one Indian legend, and the mortal remains of an early patriot.

♦ That to the die-hard Yankees of northern New England everything south of Hartford is the Deep South; that to the apartment dwellers of Manhattan there is nothing to the west of the Hudson River save open range and an occasional used-car lot, and that a Texan's view of the rest of the nation is of a right and left coast that run just beyond either side of Oklahoma.

♦ That citizens in the eastern United States have a keen interest in forest fires in remote regions of the American West, a curiosity understood and fulfilled by the persons who produce hourly newscasts on the radio networks.

♦ That there is, to this day, a community of women in the southern states, naturally generations removed from direct involvement in the Civil War, whose lives are marked by passionate, overwhelming hatred of Yankees.

(These women are not to be confused with female Boston Red Sox fans, whose lives are similarly marked.)

♦   That southern cold feels colder than northern cold.

♦   That when Northerners move south their blood thins after a few years and therefore they become less able to withstand cold.

♦   That southerners go into a catatonic trance at the smell of fried chicken or the sound of Johnny Cash's voice.

♦   That all of Dixie spends Saturday night either listening to the Grand Ole Opry on the radio or watching a demolition derby.

♦   That every small southern town contains an intelligent and quietly liberal lawyer who is "sensible" on the racial issue and thus a credit to his race when written about in eastern journals.

♦   That the Rocky Mountain states are populated by two kinds of people: mellow young environmentalists who always wear plaid shirts and jeans and know John Denver personally, and old-timers with faces as craggy as the mountains.

♦   That there is a sign you see as you leave California and enter Oregon. It reads:

LEAVING CALIFORNIA—

RESUME NORMAL BEHAVIOR

♦   That southern California contains all the off-the-wall nuts and that northern California (as well as Washington and Oregon) is an Olympian, conservative, cultivated place, managed well by a few old families.

♦   That there is no body of beliefs so bizarre that it does not have an active cult following in the southwest corner of the nation.

Rich People, Poor People, Etc.

◆ That all inherited wealth represents Grandpa's ill-gotten gains; that all rich people are unhappy; that all rich people marry five times and raise miserable children because they don't know the secret of a happy life, which is readily obtainable from any passing factory worker.

◆ That all persons of great wealth or responsibility secretly pine for the simple life.

◆ That the rural poor are somehow less miserable than the urban poor.

◆ That illiterate people sign their names by making large, crude *X*'s.

(Most illiterate people have created signatures for themselves; the X's show up in fiction and in movies.)

◆ That the people who were most popular in high school amount to nothing in later life. The "nerds" from high school become highly successful.

◆ That people who get up early are of generally better character than those who get up late.

◆ That silent people tend to be deep thinkers.

◆ That pipe smokers are lousy tippers and deliberate excessively when making a purchase.

◆ That primitive people have good teeth and cannot get lost in the wilderness.

◆ That there are thousands of safety deposit boxes in banks around the country crammed full of cash and jewelry left by long-deceased actors and eccentrics; if converted to public use, these riches would reduce the deficit by upwards of 15 percent.

◆   That despite what sociologists, journalists, and others have reported, there are great numbers of Americans who are quite content with dull, repetitive, and demeaning jobs.

◆   That if the total wealth of the United States were equally divided among all citizens, five years thereafter we would be back to the same unequal division we have now, with control of the wealth in largely the same hands as today.

Science, Technology, and Nature

◆   That new technology always takes five years to develop, the only exception being during World War II, when things were developed and put into production and service almost overnight.

◆   That perpetual motion is a goal worth striving for, as it will bring about great benefits to mankind.

◆   That at some indefinite point in the future we will live in energy-efficient domed solar cities, move about on monorails, and wear togas.

◆   That the main earthly effect of the space program has been to change the weather.

◆   That scientists are motivated by a search for the truth, except for those involved in technology, who are interested only in the buck.

◆   That after a scientist wins a Nobel, he or she is so famous and is in such demand for speeches, articles, appearances, and interviews that he or she never does any more serious research.

◆ That there are an infinite number of ways of using statistics as a means to deceive.

◆ That it is darkest just before dawn.

(It is darkest about two A.M.)

◆ That computers do not make errors. That only humans make computer errors.

(Anyone who believes this has never been around when a disk in a PC "crashes" or turns bad.)

◆ That there is no such thing as a straight line in nature.

(Ever see a crystal formation?)

◆ That American science and technology get moving only when confronted by an outside threat (Pearl Harbor, Sputnik, the Arab oil embargo).

◆ That warm water freezes faster than cold water.

(The redoubtable Ann Landers got into an ongoing row with readers in 1983 when she addressed this question, as well as the related cosmic issue of whether cold water boils faster than hot water. She "went to the top" and consulted Dr. Jereome Weisner, chancellor of the Massachusetts Institute of Technology, who kicked the problem over to the MIT dean of science, Dr. John W. Deutch. Landers never recorded what Deutch thought of being given such a problem by an advice column, but the eminent scientist reported, "Neither statement was true." Whereupon "Self-Reliant in Riverdale" (in a Landers column that ran in The Washington Post on July 27, 1983) upbraided her for using "argument by authority" rather than doing her own experiment. "Self-Reliant" said she reached the same conclusion as Deutch by using a pan of hot water, a thermometer, a stove, a refrigerator, and a watch with a second hand. We think it would be simpler to write MIT, as Landers did.)

◆ That nature abhors a vacuum.

(The universe is mostly empty space, after all; we live in a vacuum.)

◆ That there is global warming and that we are due for another ice age.

(These are the two predominant views of the environmental future: one or both must be wrong.)

◆ That it is possible to divine for water with a forked willow branch. If, however, the dip of the branch indicates an area that is dry, it means only that the divining was done improperly or by an inexperienced diviner.

♦ That still waters run deep.

(How can still water run?)

♦ That moss grows only on the north side of trees.

♦ That there is such a thing as an air pocket, which is a bane of air travel.

(There is a downdraft; but it is no pocket.)

♦ That if you hold a seashell to your ear you can hear the roar of the ocean. You should bring at least a dozen shells home each time you visit the shore.

(The sound you hear actually comes from sounds around you that are picked up and intensified in the inner spaces of the shell. One of the sounds picked up and amplified is that of blood rushing through your ear.)

♦ That it is possible for the average person to get a poinsettia to bloom for a second Christmas.

♦ That an American patent commissioner resigned in the early nineteenth century because there was nothing new left to invent.

(Librarian/critic Sam Sass has written of this in The Berkshire Eagle:

One of my favorite myths, which appears regularly in the scientific literature; I even read it as a fact not long ago in the *Saturday Review*. That's the story about the official of the U.S. Patent Office who resigned because he believed that there was nothing left to invent.

I was once asked by a GE scientist to track down the origin of that tale. I found that the source was a sentence in the 1843 annual report of the commissioner of patents: "The advancement of the arts, from year to year, taxes our credulity and seems to presage the arrival of that period when human improvement must end." That man did not resign until a few years later, and not because he thought there was nothing left for him to do. In fact, he made plans for the long-term future of the Patent Office. Thus, on a single rhetorical sentence was built a myth that has been repeated for nearly a century and a half.

SHOW BUSINESS

~~~~~

- That a single negative review in *The New York Times* can kill a Broadway show after one night; that if the *Times* had been around to review Shakespeare, English teachers would be teaching another playwright today.
- That a cabal of five advertising executives dictates the content of prime-time viewing on the three major networks. They are fearful that new ideas might disturb viewers; hence the repetitive quality of what Americans are forced to watch.
- That cable television has vast but unspecified potential to deliver more than six-month-old movies, commercial-free reruns of *Dick Van Dyke,* home shopping, and the Atlanta Hawks games.
- That people who claim they watch only documentaries on television never miss an episode of *Married With Children* or *Roseanne.*
- That a number of female movie stars of the period from approximately 1930 through 1960 were discovered at the counter of Schwab's Pharmacy at Sunset Boulevard and Laurel.

  (The actress most often mentioned as being "discovered" in the drugstore was Lana Turner. But an Associated Press dispatch from Los Angeles [printed in The New York Times *and other papers on October 27, 1983] stated: "The legend of Miss Turner's film career being started at Schwab's has no traceable source and is denied by Miss Turner, now 63 years old. But Mr. [Leon] Schwab, who spent more than 51 years at the drugstore, recalls a story concerning another famous person, this one involving Charlie Chaplin. Mr. Schwab said the comic used to get behind the soda fountain and make his own milkshakes.")*

- That it is bad luck to wish an actor good luck.
- That in defiance of the nutritional laws governing the health of more mundane mortals, rock stars can subsist indef-

initely on a diet of cocaine and M&M candies. Most of them, however, come to tragic ends at an early age, and remain alive as immortals in their fans' memories for as long as three weeks.

◆ That if you are a man and are going to appear on TV you should wear a blue shirt (never a white one.)

◆ That the only westerns worth watching are *Stagecoach* and *High Noon.*

◆ That all jokes heard on *Late Night with David Letterman,* in Las Vegas lounges, at last week's PTA meeting, or wherever derive from *Joe Miller's Jests* of 1739.

◆ That bad times are best for the movie business, as people throng to adventures and musicals to forget their problems.

◆ That all film stars and rock stars live miserable, dissipated lives.

◆ That utterly fascinating and fantastic conversations take place in the "green rooms" of television talk shows, which are interrupted so that less interesting conversations can take place in front of the camera.

◆ That the world's leading pop songs occur to the composer while he is showering or making love, and are converted into final-score form within twenty minutes or so.

◆ That in order to amount to anything as a comedian in America you must have been born in Brooklyn or in a small town in the Midwest.

◆ That good conversation, especially among families, has been drowned out by television.

(This replaces the belief that it was drowned out by radio, which replaces the belief that it was drowned out by the stereoscope.)

SPACE

◆ That humans would be incapable of dealing with beings from elsewhere in space and the yahoos among us would shoot them on sight if they ever landed on earth.

◆ That there are canals on Mars.

◆ That NASA has discovered the existence of a "lost day" but is hiding the fact from the public.

(This belief is so widely held that the space agency includes the following disclaimer in "This is NASA," the basic pamphlet it uses to describe its activities: "There is no truth to the recurring story that NASA uncovered a 'lost day' in the movement of the Earth. Although planetary positions are used to help determine spacecraft orbits, we have been unable to learn of any computations in the space program which revealed a 'lost day,' as has been reported in a number of places.")

◆ That it was easier to land astronauts on the moon than it is to cleanse a polluted river.

◆ That the National Aeronautics and Space Administration has made unimagined discoveries that it is now hiding for fear of widespread panic.

◆ That most of the people who report UFO sightings live in or near swamps and seldom comb their hair.

◆ That if a Ph.D. scientist sees a UFO he is immediately given a large "grant" from the Air Force or National Security Agency in exchange for his silence.

Sports

◆ That tennis balls contain poisonous gas.

(Other versions maintain that it is honey or Karo syrup. None of this is true; liquid-center balls contain water or a mild oil.)

◆ That an athlete should not engage in sex the night before a big game.

◆ That Abner Doubleday invented baseball and that it was first played in Cooperstown, New York.

(The Doubleday myth stemmed in part from the desire of the early pooh-bahs of baseball to prove that their sport was American in origin. Among other points that have been made in disproving the

myth is that Doubleday was at West Point when he was supposedly in Cooperstown inventing the game. In fact, there is no proof that he was ever in Cooperstown. It actually evolved from English cricket and rounders as well as other hybrid American games of the early 1800s.)

◆ That if a baseball pitcher is working on a no-hitter, no mention should be made of it lest he be jinxed.

◆ That any male American knows how to keep score at a baseball game; he knows the fine points of all the rules of all major American sports and can explain them to his wife, who won't understand them anyway.

◆ That ballpark food *will not* make you sick.

◆ That it is a great and noble thing for a man to take his son to a baseball game.

◆ That a baseball player whose sensational play provides the third out in an inning is always the leadoff hitter when his team comes to bat.

◆ That even when the Chicago Cubs won their last pennant in 1945, it wasn't worth much, since all but the halt and the lame were at war.

◆ That the people who make baseball cards hold back on superstars so that in order to get a Dave Winfield or a Jose Canseco you have to buy five nobodies from the Cubs or Mariners.

◆ That if the leadoff batter strikes out, that team will lose the game.

◆ That all of those people you see at a baseball game on TV are actually trying to *catch* that screaming line drive foul ball hit into their section.

(As anyone who has been there would know, the possible concussion or broken bones that would follow are not worth the souvenir).

◆ That a curve ball does not curve at all; that this is an optical illusion.

(A spinning ball curves in both practice and theory.)

◆ That boxing is still the surest and fastest ticket from poverty to fame and fortune.

◆ That a city with a winning National Football League team loses 7.1 hours of work time weekly per capita in water-cooler discussions about the last and next week's games.

◆ That a city with a losing National Football League team

loses 7.1 hours of work time weekly per capita in water-cooler discussions about the last and next week's games.

♦ That cities without National Football League teams are populated by men who lose 7.1 hours of work time weekly in water-cooler discussions about the local high school or college season.

♦ That it's more fun to be at a football game in a raging snowstorm with the temperature hovering at 0° than to watch the same game on TV in the comfort of your own warm home.

♦ That quarterbacks and even offensive guards in the National Football League keep in their heads intricate plays and assignments that are beyond the comprehension of Princeton mathematicians; once off the field, however, they must read cue cards to get through beer commercials.

♦ That the best football players come from Texas or Pennsylvania.

♦ That significant numbers of American men do away with themselves on the Sunday afternoons just after the Super Bowl.

♦ That a number of our leading stock-car drivers learned how to drive from running corn liquor and evading revenuers on mountain roads.

(The kernel of truth behind this credo is the fact that Junior Johnson, crew manager for Cale Yarborough, Darrell Waltrip, and other champions of the National Association of Stock Car Auto Racing in fact served time in a federal prison for hauling moonshine.)

♦ That if you are having a great day fishing and decide to stop and count your catch, your luck will evaporate and you will be fortunate to catch even one more.

♦ That fish bite only at sunset and dawn.

♦ That the fishing is especially good when the cattle are grazing.

♦ That a young child or old man fishing with crude equipment and worms will always reach his limit before a man with the latest and most expensive gear.

♦ That one can draw successfully to fill an inside straight.

♦ That if you are lucky at cards you will be unlucky in love.

♦ That a backwoods logger or big-bellied trucker is the worth of several karate experts in a fight.

♦ That the basketball player to make the last basket during warm-up will have a good game.

♦ That white men can't jump.

♦ That in golf you drive for show and putt for dough.

♦ That from time to time a golfer who will not leave the links despite the imminence of an electrical storm will be hit by lightning. The intrepid golfer will be unharmed, but his clubs will melt.

♦ That when teeing off in golf you should place the ball so that the brand name is up. If it is not up, you will lose the hole.

♦ That South American soccer fans are an irrational, temperamental lot—unlike the people who go to watch American college and professional football.

♦ That "close" counts only in horseshoes.

♦ That chess is excellent discipline for the mind—far superior to television or reading.

♦ That the America's Cup race is an exciting event provided you understand all the nuances of sailing.

♦ That people who can water-ski find it easy to snow-ski; and the reverse.

♦ That jogging is beneficial both physically and spiritually, and any day now we are going to give it a try; that anyone past age thirty-five should consult a physician before undertaking so strenuous a sport, and that next week, or maybe the next, we intend to ask the doctor about it; that in the interim we are reading a book by Jack Kennedy's back doctor on the health-enhancing qualities of rocking chairs.

♦ That the Baby Ruth candy bar was named for slugger Babe Ruth.

(Actually it was named for President Grover Cleveland's daughter Ruth.)

♦ That a team or individual athlete will be jinxed during the week they appear on the cover of *Sports Illustrated*.

♦ That playing softball will hurt one's ability to play baseball.

TRANSPORTATION

◆ That the best way to avoid heavy traffic on roads connecting our cities with the ocean resorts is to leave before seven o'clock in the morning, save for those instances when intuition says the slack period will be at midday because everyone else left early; that traffic departments of rural hamlets en route create congestion to force motorists to purchase vast quantities of soft ice cream and gasoline; that the sea nettles weren't this prevalent three summers ago; that another half hour in the sun won't do any harm; that as long as you keep moving around in the sun and swimming, you can drink two or three times as much beer as normal without feeling a thing; that you are entitled to do so anyway, because this is summer and you are on vacation.

◆ That foreign cars are better built than domestic ones.

◆ That a carburetor has been invented that results in a passenger car's getting fifty to seventy-five miles per gallon. However, the rights to the unit were purchased by General Motors and/or Ford and/or the Japanese and/or the Germans, who is (are) keeping the invention a secret.

◆ That you are more likely to get a lemon if you buy a car manufactured on Monday or Friday.

◆ That if you take driver education when you are young you will be a safer driver the rest of your life.

(Not so, according to the results of the National Highway Traffic Safety Administration study released in 1981. "No statistically significant difference" in accident rates was found between those who had or had not taken driver education.)

◆ That if you kick the tires of a used car, the salesman will know he'd better not try to hoodwink you about the value of the car.

◆ That you can "find yourself" through travel.

(Writing on this belief in the "My Turn" section of Newsweek, *William J. Bennett says, "The harder one looks for The Answer in faraway places, the more elusive and distant it becomes. Wherever and whatever The Answer is [if it is anywhere at all], it tends not to be found on cruises.")*

◆ That if you give an airline hostess a twenty-dollar bill for a drink, she won't be able to make change, thereby providing you a free drink.

◆ That although airline stewardesses were wild and crazy lassies only a few years ago, bent mainly on seducing and possibly marrying wealthy business travelers, most of them now are settled family types devoted to their children, old-fashioned morality, and the pursuit of the classical cello. That the real swingers among them now work on private corporate jets, aboard which unspeakable practices are performed at altitudes of four miles or more. An ever-widening circle of stewardesses who have had sex aloft are said to be members of the "mile high" club.

◆ That the nation's railroads successfully conspired to bring about such a rapid decline in passenger service that it forced the government to step in and create Amtrak.

◆ That it is unthinkable to sail on a ship that has not been properly christened.

◆ That Volkswagens will float for an indefinite amount of time.

◆ That the captain of a sinking ship goes down with the ship or—at the very least—is the last one to leave the vessel.

(In August 1991 as the Greek liner Oceanos *was sinking off the coast of South Africa, the captain made it off on the first helicopter, elbowing aside the elderly and leaving 170 astonished passengers on the ship. David Streifeld of* The Washington Post *investigated this story and reported that—much to the surprise of many—there is no law that requires a captain to stay with his passengers, let alone stay with the ship until it sinks. Nor is there anything in maritime law that insists that women and children are the first to be allowed off the sinking vessel.)*

War Rumors—
Gossip Goes to
Battle

A. URBAN MYTHS IN WARTIME

As the Burmese diplomat U Thant opined while secretary general of the United Nations during the 1960s, "As you know, in times of war and of hostilities the first casualty is truth."

Rumor, however, flourishes—the Urban Myth Gone to War, if you will. When the guns begin to roar every government tries to control what its people are told, both to maintain popular support for its policies and to deny information to the adversary. At the same time, a government busily spreads disinformation and nonsense to the other side, attempting to deceive its military and to demoralize its citizenry.

With normal communications channels constricted, and government deliberately withholding or doctoring the news, little wonder that wartime provides a lush growth climate for urban myths.

During World War I, harmful domestic rumors became so rampant that an official campaign was launched to track them to their sources and attempt rebuttal. The work was done by the American Protective League, a quasi-official organization of amateur snoops that worked under the Justice Department. Sadly, the APL pooh-bahs seemed to know little of the self-generating quality of rumors: to the APL, the fact that a nasty report was circulating meant that it was "enemy propaganda" started by the detested Huns.

The APL national office in Washington sent a circular to its field offices in January 1918 warning: "Stories of the most fanciful character have been invented to destroy faith and confidence in the honesty of the Government and in the agencies conducting the war." Then the APL violated the first rule of rumor-quelching by listing some of the claimed instances of "enemy propaganda" that it said had been circulating: "Epidemics, scenes of terrible suffering in the camps, overfeeding and underfeeding of troops, graft in the Fuel and Food Administration, the same of Red Cross supplies, the wasting of public monies, and worst of all, the letters coming from the front telling of serious losses to our men, sea disasters and untold hardships."

The APL asked for reports on rumors "most widespread through your district" and whether any had been "traced to German sources." The APL was promptly deluged with versions of The Mother's Sweater Story. The account from the APL office in New York City was typical:

A friend of mine told me that a friend of hers made a sweater for her boy and addressed it to his regiment. He never received the same. This woman put a twenty-dollar bill in the sleeve of the sweater, so that her boy would be surprised when he found same. Imagine what happened. This woman was passing a certain street and noticed this sweater in a window for sale. She recognized it by a peculiar cross stitch that she makes, and walking in demanded the sweater, proving her claim to same by finding the twenty-dollar bill still in the arm of the sweater.

The APL office in Kansas City, Missouri, had a slightly different version: that a woman made a sweater "for the soliders" and that "in the pocket of this sweater she had pinned a letter telling her name and address and wishing success to the wearer." A soldier wrote to her "telling her that the sweater was a good one, but it had cost him eight dollars." From Pierre, South Dakota, came the same story, the report adding, "This story seems to be pretty general over the northwest but

I do not know where it started from. The majority of people laugh at it and know that it is a falsehood but it will work with a certain class of people, make them lose confidence in the work of the Red Cross." The APL chief in Troy, New York, gave his version, and said he "was informed that the story was heard in Pittsfield (60 miles from here) in identically the same form." In Tucson the mother marked the sweater with initials rather than money or a note but nonetheless found it for sale in a shop.

Another rumor reported nationwide concerned President Woodrow Wilson's private secretary, Joseph Tumulty. Informants excitedly told APL agents that he had been convicted of treason and was either executed or imprisoned at Leavenworth. (Totally false: Tumulty remained at Wilson's side until the end of his presidency.)

Stories abounded about "insufficient food and heat at training camps," hospitals full of burned survivors of naval disasters, an imminent collapse of values of War Bonds, and "stories that war would end in revolution and that German soliders would patrol streets of Cincinnati."

R. A. Gunn, director of the APL office in Chicago, was one of the few field agents who denied credit for any of this alarm to German propagandists. "The rumors," he wrote, "are spread through the ordinary channels of gossip."

At a cabinet meeting on October 16, 1918, the subject of rumors of German "atrocities" arose. Secretary of the Navy Josephus Daniels wrote: "[Secretary of War Newton D.] Baker said he heard many stories of cruelty and barbaric actions by Germans. The Army traced them down and found only 2 of many cases true.

"Generally a man had heard that it happened in another regiment. Stories of [German] cruelty and stories of our cruelty are exaggerated. One American soldier did shoot a German prisoner of war in the back but they found he was crazy."

President Woodrow Wilson remarked, "Men tell stories they say happened to them to make it more personal when it was only a rumor they adopted."

B. CONFUSE THY ENEMY

The Office of Strategic Services, created early during World War II, was an intelligence service that more or less created its own functions. Well stocked with Madison Avenue ad salesmen and psychologists turned spooks, the OSS recognized early the value—and techniques—of effective psychological warfare in which rumor was used to undermine the morale of the enemy. According to an OSS manual: "Rarely can [rumors] by themselves change basic attitudes. Their function is to confirm suspicions and beliefs already latent; to give sense and direction to fears, resentments or hopes that have been built up by more materialistic causes; to tip the balance when public opinion is in a precarious state."

The manual's section entitled "Properties of a Good Rumor" is a virtual definition of a good urban myth as well.

A good rumor is one that will spread widely in a form close to that of the original story. Probably the main factor determining whether or not it catches on is the degree to which it is adapted for the state of mind of the audience. In addition, successful rumors embody most of the following qualities:

1. *Plausibility.* A plausible rumor is tied to some known facts, yet is incapable of total verification. It may exaggerate, but it stops short of the incredible. It frequently appears as an "inside" story.

2. *Simplicity.* A good rumor uses only one central idea as a core. Its basic message is simple and thus easy to remember.

3. *Suitability to task.* To summarize opinions or attitudes that are already widely accepted, slogan-type rumors are best. ("England will fight to the last Frenchman.") To introduce "information" that will help build up new attitudes, however, narrative-type rumors are best (e.g., rumors that "prove" Hitler was mentally ill).

4. *Vividness.* Regardless of length or type, rumors that stimulate clear-cut mental pictures with strong emotional content are likely to be effective.

5. *Suggestiveness.* The type of rumor that merely hints or suggests something instead of stating it is well adapted to spreading fear and doubt. The listener should always be allowed to formulate his own conclusions.

6. *Concreteness.* The more concrete and precise a rumor, the less likely it is to become distorted in transmission.

As experience whetted its expertise at rumormongering, the "Morale Division" of OSS by 1944 had devised formal subcategories for the various notions it was floating into Nazi Germany and Occupied Europe. Here are some examples of OSS files in the National Archives in Washington:

THE CONFUSION RUMOR

Inciting fear of inflation is the most direct road to creating inflation. Working on this principle, the Morale Division started three rumors:

- *"The Reichsdruckerei [the German Mint] is printing large quantities of currency."*
- *"The value of the [German] mark in the black markets of Switzerland has dropped considerably."*
- *"Life insurance companies have asked the [German] government for extensive emergency loans. Because of the large number of deaths in the Reich, these companies are no longer solvent."*

THE DECEPTION RUMOR

During the summer of 1944, marketplace rumors were planted in Eastern Europe to the effect that all German troops were withdrawing from the Crimea, "leaving all Romanians behind to be annihilated." Within days angry Romanian women demonstrated outside the Bucharest home of their president, demanding, "Send our husbands home."

THE PERSONAL GOSSIP ATTACK RUMOR

OSS played with many variants of the theme "Where is Hitler?" OSS would state in its own broadcasts and through neutral press leaks that Hitler was expected to speak at a Nazi anniversary celebration and give the time and place of the affair—an event solely of OSS's creation. When Hitler "did not appear," OSS would then circulate reports of his "rumored death, disappearance, illness, psychotic condition, or flight from the country." The purpose was to "sow doubt in the minds of the public and the Wehrmacht, and cast suspicions on the motive and integrity of the Nazi leadership." These rumors so unnerved the Nazis that they tried a countermeasure to deflate them. The propaganda minister, Joseph Goebbels, claimed over Radio Berlin on December 29, 1944, that he had "purposely planted rumors that Hitler was ill as a part of a deep and far-flung scheme to lull the Allies into complacency and set them up for the winter offensive." Goebbels' broadcast confirmed to the OSS that its tactic was succeeding.

THE HUMOROUS RUMOR

On June 16, 1943, OSS had its agents in Occupied Europe circulate the quip, "Barbers in Holland are now charging five cents more for a shave, because German faces are longer these days."

Within two months the rumor had jumped back across the Atlantic to Rhode Island. The *Providence Journal* reported on August 25, 1943: "A Dutch underground newspaper reports that the barbers of Germany are now charging five cents extra to shave Nazis because their faces are longer these days."*

THE PIPE-DREAM RUMOR

These OSS rumors promised a better life to Axis soldiers who surrendered. A leaflet given to Germans in North Africa maintained that POWs lived in near-luxury, with such assignments as driving limousines for Allied generals. Several captured German airmen who inquired about getting such jobs were disappointed.

---

*For a planted report to be reprinted as true in the domestic press of an intelligence organization's country is known as "blow back." William Colby, the director of central intelligence, told a Senate committee in 1977 that this often happens when CIA plants material in foreign newspapers; his attitude was that "blow back" was an unavoidable by-product of covert operations.

THE BOGEYMAN RUMOR

Harking to the tumultuous ending of World War I, the OSS and British intelligence broadcast "reports" that the German navy would be forced to make a final suicidal attack against the British Isles. A similar report in the early fall of 1918 caused the German navy to mutiny, helping bring the conflict to an end. World War II ended before this particular rumor had time to have any effect.

THE WEDGE-DRIVING RUMOR

These nasties exploit religious, racial, and other prejudices, and there are hundreds in OSS archives. Two illustrations of the genre:

"At a dinner recently held at Karin Hall by Göring, beer was served in sacred vessels looted from churches in Northern Italy."

"To save time and space, Himmler has ordered no distinction be observed in cremations of Protestant and Catholic air-raid victims."

World War II Interlude

• That the Japanese had poor vision and would be worthless as fighter pilots.
(This was a cherished myth of the period and in part responsible for the fact that so many Japanese were caricatured with thick glasses.)
• That most Japanese armament was made from American scrap metal, and the familiar logos of U.S. auto companies could occasionally be found on artillery shells.
• That if the American people ever learned the real truth about Pearl Harbor, President Roosevelt would have been impeached.
(New evidence published by historian John Toland in his 1982 book Infamy *suggests [but does not emphatically prove] that the suspicions*

were well founded: that FDR did in fact know of the Japanese plans in advance of the attack.)

• That the average German officer wore a monocle and a gray greatcoat, and rode around the battlefield in an open touring car, clicking his heels smartly at the sight of a superior.

• That German submarines regularly sank convoys of American ships only a few miles off the U.S. coast, and residents could see them burning on the horizon; censorship prevented this news from appearing in print.

• That the Pentagon was staffed exclusively by armchair commandos who had priority for Scotch whiskey rations, gave silk stockings to their blonde girlfriends, and relied on old college classmates to keep them out of battle.

• That during World War II, (a) all Japanese officers above the rank of captain spoke fluent, if slightly accented, English, and graduated from UCLA; (b) no Japanese soldier could pronounce "Babe Ruth"; they all said "Babe Luth," so the baseball player's name was frequently used as a password by troops on the front line; (c) German soldiers disguised as American GIs could always be exposed by asking them the name of Li'l Abner's girlfriend. "Lilly Marlene" was not the correct answer.

• That an American imprisoned in a Japanese POW camp sent his mother a letter stating that he was being treated well and asking her to save the stamp for his collection. The request surprised the mother, because the soldier was not a collector. She managed to steam off the stamp, and she found written under it: "They have cut off my tongue."

(In terms of repetition, this was one of the more widely circulated rumors of World War II, even though POW mail from neither side bore stamps.)

• That U.S. and Allied bombers were prohibited from bombing certain factories in Germany because they actually belonged to the Rockefellers, General Motors, Ford, etc.

• That when American soliders captured some factories in Germany they were packed with brand-new American-made machinery that American companies sold to the Germans via Spain.

• That American bombers were prohibited from bombing the

financial district in Tokyo because of American interests in banks and other companies there, and because General MacArthur wanted a fancy big building for his headquarters.

("Actually," writes Bob Skole, who was there for the occupation, "the financial district was not much damaged because Toyko was fire-bombed and the district's buildings were mainly brick and concrete. Besides, it was very close to the Imperial Palace, which was indeed prohibited from being bombed. The nearby Tokyo central railway station, however, was badly damaged. MacArthur did use the Dai Ichi Building headquarters of a big insurance company for his headquarters. It is just across the moat from the Royal Palace. Interesting point in this, and illustrating inaccuracy of bombing, is that the Imperial Guard Barracks, a huge five-story concrete building that I figure was the size of a football field, was not hit at all, even though everything around it was flattened. I was stationed with the Eighth Cavalry Regiment in that building in the occupation. The bombers certainly did not save it for us, although it was nice for us they missed it.")

WEATHER

◆ That animals instinctively know more about impending weather conditions than humans. (Bears, for instance, will grow thicker coats in anticipation of a particularly severe winter, while squirrels will put away an especially large supply of nuts.)

◆ That birds instinctively know more about impending weather conditions than humans. (A sea gull inland means that a big storm is on its way.)

◆ That insects instinctively know more about impending weather conditions than humans. (Woolly caterpillars, for example, foretell the severity of the coming winter. The wider the middle band of light brown, the milder the winter.)

♦ That there is such a thing as earthquake weather—that is, a meteorological tip-off.

(Charles Moss of Los Angeles reports that this is a commonly held belief in his part of the world, where any stretch of similar weather—cold, hot, wet—is regarded by many as "earthquake weather.")

♦ That vegetables instinctively know more about impending weather conditions than humans. (A thick cornhusk, for instance, indicates a cold winter is on the way. Onions know a lot, too:

**Onion's skin very thin
Mild winter coming in.
Onion's skin thick and tough
Coming winter cold and rough.)**

♦ That the annual appearance of the groundhog on February 2 provides a more accurate forecast of the spring climate than any other of those fancy dials and instruments purchased at great cost by the U.S. Weather Service; that no newspaper has ever done a systematic study of the accuracy of the groundhog's prediction for fear the findings will deprive editors of an annual front-page story and funny picture.

♦ That it never rains as much as on weekends.

♦ That the *Farmer's Almanac* invariably does a better job of predicting weather than scientifically based government and private forecasters.

(Writer Bill Tague compared the Almanac's *predictions with real winter in the February 1983 issue of* Berkshire Winter *and concluded that these prognostications were "nothing but hokum and bosh.")*

♦ That dampness makes arthritis get worse.

♦ That your blood will thin after living a year in a hot, humid climate such as Florida.

(The consistency of one's blood remains constant whether one is living in Alaska or Florida. Heatstroke will cause a temporary thinning, however.)

♦ That it can get too cold to snow.

♦ That Eskimos have a number of words for snow—more than 100, according to some experts.

(This myth has taken on such monumental proportions that a book was published in 1991 entitled The Great Eskimo Vocabulary Hoax, *by Geoffery K. Pullum, to silence these claims and point out that Eskimos don't actually have any more words for snow than anyone else.)*

◆ That no two snowflakes are alike.

(Much evidence dispels this improbable myth. But nothing is quite so compelling as this from the "Science Notebook" section of the June 20, 1988, Washington Post:

There are two snowflakes alike, and Nancy C. Knight has found them.

The discovery of the first matching pair of snowflakes was reported in the May issue of the Bulletin of the American Meteorological Society.

Knight, of the National Center for Atmospheric Research in Boulder, Colorado, reported collecting the snowflakes in a research flight over Wausau, Wisconsin. During that flight a glass slide was exposed briefly to pick up crystals.

◆ That when snowflakes start getting big it means that the snow will soon stop.

◆ That the worst snowstorms are always missed by the forecasters, and that many heart attacks take place as homeowners shovel "flurries" from their driveways.

◆ That a ring around the moon is a sure sign of rain or snow.

◆ That if you see a cat eating grass it is a sure sign of rain.

◆ That dogs eat grass and cats sneeze just before rain.

◆ That early freezing foretells a mild winter. Or, as expressed in a very old couplet:

Ice in November to bear a duck
The rest of the winter will be but muck.

◆ That it's not the heat that gets to you, it's the humidity.

◆ That there are people who can predict the weather by paying attention to their corns, their lumbago, or some other bodily forecaster.

◆ That lightning never strikes twice in the same place.

(According to the Chicago Tribune *the Empire State Building was struck forty-eight times in a single year. It can also strike the same person more than once. There is the widely reported case of the late Roy C. Sullivan, "the human lightning conductor." Here is the record as related by Michael Kernan in* The Washington Post *in 1986: "Sullivan, for years a ranger in Shenandoah National Park in Virginia, was struck seven times over 35 years. On different occasions he: lost his big toenail; burned off his eyebrows; seared his left shoulder; caught his hair on fire; injured his ankle; and was hospitalized with chest burns.*

"On August 7, 1973, when he was driving his car—for anybody else, the safest place to be in a thunderstorm—a bolt knocked his hat off and set his hair on fire again, blew him clear out of the car, whipped through both legs and took off his left shoe.

"He had to put out the fire on his head with a pail of water. The hat is in a Guinness World Records exhibit hall. Sullivan died in 1983.")

♦   That when smoke from a chimney lies close to the ground, it will either rain or snow.

♦   That the moon is responsible for changes in the weather.

♦   That no matter what the forecast says, a newly washed car will cause it to rain.

♦   That trailer parks attract tornadoes.

(Mobile homes cannot withstand wind as well as conventional houses; hence the highly visible damage displayed in TV news shows.)

♦   That if you leave your umbrella at home, it is sure to rain.

♦   That the hue of the sky is a more accurate warning of nautical weather conditions than is the weather service, to wit:

Red sky at night,
Sailors delight.
Red sky at morning,
Sailors take warning.

THE GREAT
INERADICABLE
MODERN FABLE

~~~~~~

In the spring of 1961 one of the authors received an anguished telephone call from a colleague who reported on police matters for *The Dallas Morning News.* His information seemed solid, for it had been told to the publisher at a cocktail party the evening before by an esteemed banker. Nonetheless, the police reporter could find no verifying details. Did the story perhaps fall within the jurisdiction of the author, who at that time was monitoring happenings at the Dallas County Sheriff's Department for news of sociological and historical importance? The outline was as follows:

Several days earlier a man's car had stalled on the Central Expressway. He'd waved his arm for assistance, and a woman motorist had stopped. He explained that he thought a brief push would make his vehicle operative again and admonished, "But you must get up to about thirty-five miles an hour to do any good." The woman had nodded assent, and the man had returned to his car.

He'd waited, and waited, and fidgeted, and eventually glanced into his rearview mirror. There the woman was, bearing down on him in her car at thirty-five miles an hour.

As the police reporter explained, "The city cops don't have any record of any stalled-car accident on Central Expressway. I thought maybe it could have happened on Central in the sheriff's jurisdiction."

Well, it hadn't, as a desk sergeant stated with a guffaw when queried. "That one comes along every six months," he said. "Last time it was on Stemmons Freeway. That time the second driver was a French tourist at forty-five miles an hour."

Several months later the coauthor shifted journalistic duty stations to *The Philadelphia Inquirer.* Soon after his arrival the city editor bustled over with a grin and a page of notes. "The darnedest thing happened on the Schuylkill Expressway the other night," he said. "It seems this guy's car stalled, and . . ."

You know what else he said. Word of mouth, surely a means of communication challenging in swiftness a laser beam, had a new urban legend to disseminate around the country. Soon it would join the bathing suit that became transparent (an embarrassment that earned either $10,000 or $125,000 in damages for a woman in either Michigan, Florida, or Oregon, in a proceeding that somehow was never recorded in court records), the mouse in the pop bottle, and the black widow spider that built a nest in a woman's beehive hairdo (or was it in a hippie's unshorn locks?) and bit and killed her.

That a story is of unverifiable authenticity—a roundabout way of saying it smells to high heaven—does not restrain Americans from relishing and retelling it with their own variations and, who knows, even coming to accept it as a valid vignette of modern society. As a wizard whose name is lost to recorded history once remarked, "Never let the truth get in the way of a good story." Jan Harold Brunvand, of the University of Utah, offered a definition of the "modern urban legend" in his book *The Study of American Folklore.* He called such legends "contemporary stories in a city setting which are reported as true individual experiences, but which have traditional variants that indicate their legendary character."

Urban legends survive for years, to die out and then suddenly reappear. If a story has currency, and supposed validity, then it is told so often and with so many variations that it becomes suspect and is discarded. "The Concrete-Filled Car" is an off-again, on-again classic. Angry with his wife because of suspected infidelities, the driver of a cement transport truck happens past the house one afternoon and sees the supposed lover's car parked outside. He rolls down its windows and fills the car with three tons of wet cement. (This is the southern/

southwestern variant; in eastern states the aggrieved husband drives a fuel-oil truck; his solution is equally messy.) Sometimes this story is embellished with a kicker. The car, usually a Cadillac, is a surprise birthday present for the cement-truck driver and the man in the house is the salesman delivering the title and getting his check.

By the way, many of these stories are international. A friend of ours, the credostalking Bob Skole, reports that the cement-truck story is making the rounds in Sweden.

The long-running modern urban fable has several, if not all, of the following qualities, which contribute to its survival:

I. It contains a semblance of seemingly supportive specific detail.

The woman tries on a parka imported from Hong Kong, priced at $29.95, at a department store in a specific shopping plaza outside Hackensack, New Jersey. A viper nesting in the lining fatally bites her. Other coats are ripped apart; each is found to contain one or more vipers. An "authority on snakes" from the National Zoo in Washington, D.C., comes to the scene and declares that a "mother viper" apparently laid eggs in a pile of kapok used for the lining. Despite an attempted hush-up, word of the tragedy leaks out from the sister of an intern who was on duty at the hospital emergency room when the dying woman was brought in. None of the principals cited, of course, knows anything about any such incident—nor do they when it occurs again, in Washington, D.C., in December 1969, and the following spring in Dallas. A budding folklorist could probably build a reputation just recording the variations on this one theme: "It was actually in a pile of sweaters from Taiwan." "What I heard was, the woman wasn't dead but was in a coma and the department store has spent thousands to keep it hushed up."

Incidentally, when the Washington Star's Woody West refuted the snake story in 1969 (HOW THE PUBLIC WAS SNAKE-BITTEN BY A RUMOR), he found that his paper had gone through a lengthy investigation refuting still another snake story in the summer of 1940. Back then there was a tenacious rumor going around that a woman had been bitten by a snake at an amusement park.

II. The person who retells the yarn accepts its validity because of the source from which it comes.

A reputable journalist hears policemen in a suburban Philadelphia town laughing among themselves and is told a you-can't-print-this story. The previous evening the wife of a prominent Mainline financier hears a noise downstairs. She arouses her husband. Nude, he goes downstairs and finds water dripping into a pan beneath the sink. He bends over to investigate. The family cat happens by and takes a friendly swipe at the man's rear (or private parts). Startled, the financier arises, bumps his head, and falls to the floor unconscious. The wife telephones the police and ambulance; before they arrive, the husband awakes and tells her what happened, that the cat, not burglars, caused his bump. "But don't tell them, I'd be awfully embarrassed." In the confusion she does so anyway, and the ambulance attendants laugh so hard they drop the stretcher and break the man's arm.

When the reporter tried to verify the story, both the financier and the hospital to which he had allegedly been taken denied it. "Aha," reasoned the reporter, "a cover-up because of embarrassment." He printed it anyway, sans names. He did not know the same thing had happened a few months earlier at an American army base in Germany, with variants: a dog's cold nose, not the swipe of a cat's paw, caused a general, not a financier, to bust his head.

The Dutch mystery writer Janwillem Van de Wetering had a Netherlands version of the story in his 1976 novel *Tumbleweed,* published in paperback by Ballantine Books, to wit: A student living in a garden slept late after a night of drinking and awoke when someone rang his bell. "He didn't bother to dress so he was walking through the corridor without his clothes on. The bell was still ringing and he began to run, and his cat, a young playful animal, jumped up and took a swing at his balls. But the cat had forgotten to keep his nails in and he really got the man.

"So the man jumped up and cracked his skull on a . . . gas

pipe running along the ceiling. Somebody saw him lying in the corridor. He was bleeding and he had hurt his foot when he fell. The ambulance came and the attendants strapped him to the stretcher. He was still conscious so they asked him what happened and he told them. And then they laughed so much that they dropped the stretcher and broke his arm."

III. The story reflects contemporary fears.

Four matrons from York, Pennsylvania, although apprehensive about crime, go to New York for a shopping trip.

Their husbands warn, "If someone wants your pocketbook or jewelry, don't put up a fight. Do what they ask." The women stay at the Plaza. As they ride the elevator to breakfast, a well-dressed black man with a Doberman pinscher gets on the elevator. "Sit," he commands. The women immediately sit on the floor.

At the lobby the man asks their room number. "Ten-sixteen," one of them blurts. He nods and walks away. The other women berate her. "Now we'll have to change rooms," they say. At the desk the clerk says, "Oh, you're the ladies from 1016. Mr. Reggie Jackson thought his dog might have frightened you; he would like to pick up your checks for breakfast." Robert Curvin, pursuing this yarn for *The New York Times* in January 1982, found that the same thing had happened to an old woman in The Bronx and in an office building in midtown Manhattan. He concluded it probably began with an old Bob Newhart story in which a man enters an elevator with a large white dog and commands, "Sit, Whitey," whereupon all other occupants drop to the floor.

IV. An urban legend gains momentum from repetition in the press, even when used without names or other detail.

The dog-in-the-elevator story was on its way within days. *The Washington Post*'s "Ear" gossip column repeated it as gospel, even though the frightened York, Pennsylvania, matrons were journalistically transformed into two "mink-drenched" ladies from Washington. It was picked up in some form or other by newspapers, repeated on radio talk shows, and, after Jackson was traded, followed him to the West Coast, where it was recounted by columnist Jack Smith in the *Los Angeles Times* in 1983. "I'm evidently only a year or two late" in telling the story, Smith sheepishly wrote when readers advised him that the yarn had been around awhile. Then he told a variant which had been given to him by fellow Californian Keith D. Young, with the locale shifted from a hotel elevator to the august Houses of Parliament in London.

As Young pointed out, the British are wizards of pomp and ceremony. "Even innocent bystanders and spectators sometimes feel themselves involuntarily caught up in and reacting to the drama of the moment, though they may know little or nothing of the ritual itself. . . ." Parliament's equivalent of the U.S. Speaker of the House is called the "Keeper of the Woolsack," who wears resplendent gold-and-scarlet robes topped with a ceremonial wig. At the time of the story told by Young, the office was held by Sir Quentin Hoff, Lord Halisham.

After Parliament adjourned, Lord Halisham strode into the corridor, past an American tour group, and saw an old friend, the Honorable Neil Matten, an MP with whom he wished to speak. "Neil," Lord Halisham called. "Neil."

Young continued: "There followed an embarrassed silence, as all the tourists obediently fell to their knees."

V. There is sometimes a grain of truth to the story that adds immeasurably to its persistence.

Almost any kid growing up in America after World War II has heard something on the order of the following:

Kid A: I just heard about a Thunderbird that's for sale. It's less than a year old, loaded with all the extras, and has less than two thousand miles on it. You wanna know what they want for it?

Kid B: Jeez, I dunno, but I bet they want a lot.

Kid A: All they want is fifty bucks for it.

Kid B: You're crazy, there must be a catch.

Kid A: Okay, here's the story. The guy who owned it got real depressed one night last spring and drove it into the woods where nobody could see him and he killed himself. He laid in the car all through the summer and wasn't discovered until fall.

Now, they've tried everything, but they can't get the smell out of the car, so they want to unload it for fifty bucks.

Collectors of American folklore call this modern tale "The Death Car," and it exists in endless variations with the only constants being the cheapness of a fine car and the irremovable smell of death. The noted American folklorist Richard M. Dorson actually found a case of a real death car in a small town in Michigan. In his book *American Folklore,* Dorson asks, "Did this modern big-city legend originate with an actual incident in a hamlet of two hundred people in a rural Negro community and by the devious ways of folklore spread to Michigan's metropolises, and then to other states?" He answers, "Unlikely as it seems, the evidence from many variants, compared through the historical-geographical method of tracing folktales, calls for an affirmative answer."

VI. Formal refutation does nothing to deter the popularity of a fable.

Because of his pro-German sentiments, H. L. Mencken ceased writing about politics and contemporary events during the First World War. Whiling away his time, he wrote a spurious history of the bathtub in America, published as "A Neglected Anniversary" in the New York *Evening Mail* on December 28, 1917. In greatly documented detail Mencken told how medical doctors denounced the bathtub as "an epicurean and obnoxious toy from England, designed to corrupt the democratic simplicity of the republic . . . dangerous to the health." (Among other "authorities," Mencken cited *The Western Medical Repository* of April 23, 1843.) He concluded that President Millard Fillmore installed the first White House bathtub in January 1851. The contractor was "Harper & Gillespie, a firm of Philadelphia engineers, who proposed to furnish a tub of cast iron, capable of floating the largest man." The implied presidential endorsement ended all objections to the bathtub, popular, medical, and otherwise, Mencken wrote.

First to Mencken's amusement, then to his consternation, serious scholars here and abroad accepted his "idle jocosities" with complete seriousness. His article was cited in serious history and reference books, as well as in the press. He confessed the hoax in the *Chicago Tribune* on May 23, 1926, with some levity and the hope of burying the bogus history.

Alas, once falsehood gains a head start, truth puffs along at the rear. The *Boston Herald,* on May 23 also, printed Mencken's "confession" on page seven of its editorial section, with a four-column headline and a two-column cartoon captioned: "The American public will swallow anything." On June 13, three weeks later, the same editorial section reprinted the ten-year-old fake—"soberly and as a piece of news!" as Mencken declaimed in wonderment. He wrote a second disclaiming article for the *Tribune,* this one published on July 25, 1926. No matter, the myth raced on.

The "fact" that Fillmore installed the first presidential bathtub got into standard history books, and somehow with the first date of January 7, 1851 (Mencken had said only "early January"). TV comedian Johnny Carson used the "anniversary" for jokes twice in January 1966 in his opening monologue. A decade later three network television anchormen—Harry Reasoner, Roger Mudd, and John Chancellor—cited the "anniversary" on their evening newscasts. Incredibly, the hoax took in even such esteemed historians as Dr. Daniel J. Boorstin. In *The Americans: The Democratic Experience,* published in 1973, Boorstin wrote: "In 1851, when President Millard Fillmore reputedly installed the first permanent bathtub and water closet in the White House, he was criticized for doing something that was 'both unsanitary and undemocratic.' "

P. J. Wingate, retired vice-president of the du Pont Company and a Mencken scholar, wrote a small book on the hoax and its aftermath (*H. L. Mencken's Un-Neglected Anniversary,* published in 1980), plus articles in *The Washington Post, The Wall Street Journal, The Philadelphia Inquirer,* and elsewhere. "I had no more success in stopping the myth than did Mencken," lamented Wingate. "Serious scholars continue to use it." Indeed, the jacket of *Presidential Anecdotes,* by Dr. Paul F. Boller, Jr., published by the prestigious Oxford University Press in 1981, depicts a smiling Fillmore sitting in a bathtub, brandishing a cigar. In his text Boller (without citing a source) gives Mrs. Fillmore rather than her husband the credit: "She installed the first bathtub in the Executive Mansion (in the face of severe public criticism) and White House bathtubs have been a Presidential prerequisite ever since."

Decades after Mencken's attempts to debunk his own story, the hoax refuses to die. *The Washington Times,* incredibly, fell for the hoax twice in less than a decade. On January 26, 1983, the paper ran an article headlined: RUB A DUB DUB: THE HISTORY OF THE BATHTUB, which was an unattributed paraphrase of the HLM story. In 1992 a professor of history at The American University in Washington fell victim to the hoax, but received in good grace a chiding note from the authors and vowed never to be hoodwinked again.

Let us now assign proper credit for the first presidential bathtub. According to biographer Robert V. Remini, President Jackson had an engineer named Robert Leckie pipe water into the White House in the spring of 1833. As Remini wrote in *Andrew Jackson and the Course of American Democracy, 1833–1845* (Harper & Row, 1984), "Very soon thereafter a 'bathing room' was installed to take advantage of this running water. The room had a hot bath, a cold bath, and a shower bath, and was equipped with large copper boilers for heating the water. The location of this room is uncertain, but most probably it was placed in the basement, if not the east wing." (Remini's passage was based on research by historian William Seale, who did the definitive study of the White House, *The President's House,* published in two volumes by the White House Historical Association in 1986. Seale's book is a gold mine of information about the White House and he vows that it is barren of myth.)

In researching this chapter the authors computed that American newspapers spent 113.7 years in the past three decades chasing down spurious urban myths. (See our earlier preliminary findings in *The Western Medical Repository,* April 23, 1981.) As a guide to the city editors of the nation, and their columnists, we submit herewith a further listing of hot stories that should be discarded as soon as they arrive at the office.

For the rest of you, however, who are not city editors, sit back and enjoy these gems of modern folklore. Novelist George V. Higgins, repeating the cement-truck story in *The*

Boston Globe, makes the point: "Overlooked in the Calvinist approach, which determines the value of a true story solely by reference to the issue of whether it is in fact true, is a large category of stories for which the criterion of truth should be of no consequence whatsoever."

Great Fables

THE ADMONISHING VOICE FROM HEAVEN

An employee of a Chicago radio station glances out his window and sees a couple embracing passionately in an office building across the street. He recognizes the man as an ad executive, and knows the woman is not his wife. He telephones the man's office, and after many rings the man interrupts the lovemaking to answer. "This is God speaking," the radio employee says, "and I want you two sinners to stop that sort of conduct right now."

(In one early version the "voice from heaven" belonged to radio commentator Paul Harvey, who says that although he has heard and enjoyed the story, he has never been in a position to so speak. Other variants put the episode on a university campus in Boston and in a federal agency in Oklahoma City.)

THE BABY AND THE TURKEY

A baby-sitter waits until the parents have left and then takes LSD. Shortly thereafter she follows the instructions given to her: Put the turkey in the oven and put the baby to bed. She dutifully puts the baby in the oven and the turkey in bed.

BURYING GRANDMA

A family plans to spend its vacation in Canada on a canoe trip and decides to take Grandma, who is a spry eighty. After arriving at a remote river, the grandmother keels over dead. The local constable is notified, and he tells the family that the

paperwork associated with recording the death and shipping
the body out of the country is so great that they would be
smarter if they just packed her up and made a beeline for the
border. Taking this advice, the woman is wrapped in canvas
and strapped into the canoe, which is tied to the roof of the
family car. The family drives all day and at dark pulls into a
motel near the U.S. border. They rise early to get a fresh start
and find the car and canoe have been stolen.

(*A common P.S. to this story is that the lady is never recovered and
cannot be declared legally dead for a long time, therefore tying up her
insurance. In Duncan Emrich's* Folklore on the Land *there is another version in which the grandmother dies in the desert as the family
drives to California.*)

THE CAT AND THE SALMON

A woman cooks an elaborate salmon dish for a dinner party.
Just before guests arrive, she finds her cat nibbling at the
salmon. She tosses him out of the house and makes repairs
with the sauce. The party goes well, and everyone leaves at
midnight. While taking trash out, the woman finds the cat's
corpse in the yard. Fearing her guests ate spoiled fish, she telephones them, and they rush to the hospital for stomach pump-
ing, to their great discomfort and her great embarrassment.
The woman's next-door neighbor phones the next morning.
"I am awfully sorry. As I backed out of the driveway last night
I ran over your cat. Not wishing to ruin your dinner party, I
put his body over next to your house and decided to wait and
tell you this morning."

THE CUT-RATE JAGUAR

"Nearly new Jaguar convertible for sale, low mileage, five hundred dollars cash." Would-be buyers were there at dawn; the
first man in line handed over the money, then asked the
woman selling the car, "Why is it so cheap? This car is easily
worth ten thousand dollars."

"My husband ran away with his secretary to Las Vegas," the
woman replied. "He went broke at the dice table the first

night and wired me to sell the car and send him the money. He didn't say anything about price."

Daddy's Boots

A man is bitten by a rattlesnake whose fangs penetrate his boot. The man dies from the bite. Years later the man's son, who was a baby at the time of his father's death, finds his father's boots and decides to try them on. He feels a sharp pain in one foot and later dies. It is discovered that one of the rattler's fangs had stuck in the boot and still contained enough poison to claim the second member of the family.

The Loving But Cold Hand

The newlyweds, college students, are irked this winter morning when the car won't start. The husband says, "You walk on to class, I'll stay and tinker with the car." A few hours later she returns home and sees a pair of legs protruding from beneath the car, and hears someone working. She playfully scoops up a handful of snow, unzips the man's trousers, and gives him such a frigid surprise that his head hits the underside of the car with a clunk. She shakes him but cannot arouse him.

She runs inside to call an ambulance and finds her husband at his desk studying. "I couldn't do anything with the car," he says, "so the garage sent over a mechanic. He's working on it right now."

Manhattan White

There is a mutant strain of unbelievably potent marijuana growing in the fecund New York sewer system. Because of the lack of light, it is white and hence known variously as "New York Albino" or "Manhattan White." The strain developed as a result of thousands of users flushing their stashes down toilets as narcs closed in.

(This is, of course, a variation of the belief that flushed alligators have flourished in the New York sewers.)

THE MANIAC'S HOOK

A young couple is parked in the local lovers' lane. Suddenly—as if struck with unexplained nervousness—the girl insists that she be taken home, and the boy reluctantly agrees to leave. On the way home they turn on the car radio to hear that a one-armed homicidal maniac has just escaped from the local mental hospital. When they get to the girl's house, the boy gets out to open the door on the girl's side and finds the maniac's hook dangling from the door handle.

THE MATRON'S TV

A lady in a posh Manhattan apartment building opens her door to find a shabbily dressed man hauling off her neighbor's new color television. She asks him what he is doing, and he says that he is from a repair shop and is taking it off to be fixed. She asks the man if he could wait for a moment so that she could give him her set, which also needs fixing.

The man is, of course, a thief, and neither TV set is ever recovered.

THE NOTE FROM THE WITNESS

The woman, the victim in a rape trial, blushed when the prosecutor said, "Tell us what this man said to you when he first approached you." At her insistence the judge permitted her to write her reply on a piece of paper, which was passed to the jurors to read.

When a woman juror tried to give the paper to the man sitting next to her, he was dozing. She shook him awake. He read the note and flushed with embarrassment and hurriedly shoved it into his pocket.

"Mr. Bailiff," the judge called, "get that piece of paper from the juror and bring it here."

The juror replied in a panic, "No, sir, Your Honor, what that note says is a personal matter between this lady and me."

(This episode has been related about most courthouses in the land, but as any veteran of trials will quickly note, it contains an inherent

defect. The one witness whose testimony will not put a juror to sleep is the woman complainant in a rape case.

This story not only gets told in courthouses but occasionally pops up in newspapers. Bill Gold of The Washington Post *heard it so many times from readers of his column that he repeated it and then pointed out that it had all the earmarks of a fable. In his March 30, 1970, column, Gold says in part, "Some readers say the incident took place last week during a trial in Arlington, some say I'll find it in the records of a trial held a long time ago in Prince Georges County, one woman says she heard it from a woman who was on a jury and it happened in Washington, and a man says he had heard the story in California last year before moving here. So this one may have more miles on it than the other great 'true' story about the woman who drives away and leaves her husband stranded in his underdrawers after he has jumped out of the family trailer to find out the cause of a sudden stop.")*

THE NOTE ON THE CAR

A man returns to a shopping-center parking lot to find his new car badly damaged and the following note stuck in the windshield: THE PEOPLE WHO SAW THIS HAPPEN AND WHO ARE NOW WATCHING ME THINK THAT I AM WRITING MY NAME AND ADDRESS AND THAT OF MY INSURANCE COMPANY ON THIS NOTE. I'M NOT.

THE PHANTOM HITCHHIKER

Two guys are on their way home from a party late one rainy night and they spot a very attractive young woman standing on a street corner without a raincoat or an umbrella. They offer her a ride, she hops in the backseat and gives them her address. One of the guys gives her his jacket because she looks so cold and wet. As they near her house, one of the guys turns around to double-check the address with her and is astonished to find that she has vanished. Dumbfounded, they decide to drive to the address that she had given them. They knock, and an older woman comes to the door. They begin telling her what has happened, and she interrupts.

"That was my daughter. She was killed on the corner where you picked her up. It happened two years ago on a night like this. She's done this several times since the accident."

The next morning the two young men verify the accident in the obituary file at the local paper. The obituary notes where she was buried and they decide to visit the grave. When they arrive they find the missing jacket draped over the tombstone.

(In his book American Folklore, *Richard Dorson reports that this story has been reported over a hundred times by folklorists. "It is found as far as Hawaii," he writes, "where a rickshaw supplants the auto, and is traced back to the nineteenth century, in America, Italy, Ireland, Turkey, and China with a horse and wagon picking up the benighted traveler.")*

THE POODLE IN THE MICROWAVE

A woman bathes her pet poodle and, in a hurry to dry it, decides to pop the animal in her new microwave oven for a few seconds. The poodle explodes.

THE SECOND BLUE BOOK

The late folklorist Duncan Emrich, an academician himself, delighted in chasing down variants of an account of what he called "very clever trickery at final exam time at college." The standard tale (which Professor Lew Girdler of San Jose State College, an Emrich contributor, dates to the 1930s at the University of California at Berkeley) goes as follows:

A student with an A average faces two essay questions on his final exam, the first of which completely stumps him. He jots random thoughts into his first blue book, then labels the second book "II" and begins with what appears to be the last sentence or so to the answer to the first essay question. Then he proceeds to answer the second essay question with brilliance. He turns in only the blue book marked "II."

A few days later the professor sends him a postcard notifying him of an A in the course, and apologizing for losing the first blue book.

There are other versions. The student cannot answer the first question, so he hands in a single page marked "2" and hides the other page in his notebook. Outside class he quickly looks up the answer to the first question and has a friend with a later class in the same room "find" the first page on the floor and hand it to the teacher. In still another version, the student writes a letter to his mother in the blue book, saying he finished the exam early and is killing time, and what a fine fellow the professor is. He hands in the blue book with the letter, hurriedly does the exam out of class, and mails the second blue book to his mother. When the instructor calls him to inquire why he handed in a letter rather than the exam, he explains he must have crossed the two books, and that he will have his mother mail back the other book, without opening the envelope.

As Professor Emrich stated, "Such deception of innocent professors is greatly to be deplored, and the ingenuity of students equally to be admired."

THE SEVERED HAND I

Several frisky medical students plan to play a trick on a nurse. They tie the severed hand from one of their laboratory cadavers to the light string in a supply room that the nurse uses. The nurse goes into the room but does not come out for a long time. One of the med students becomes impatient, walks in, and finds the light on and the nurse sitting on the floor. Her hair has turned white and she is nibbling on the hand.

SEVERED HAND II

A male medical student who commuted each day along a stretch of the Massachusetts Turnpike was trying to come up with a way to attract the attention of a sexy toll-booth attendant. He hit on the idea of taking a hand from his cadaver, attaching a quarter to the palm, and giving it to the lady in the booth. He decided to go ahead with the grisly gag, and the woman dropped dead of shock.

The Ski Accident

A woman takes a lift to the top of a ski slope, where she finds she has to relieve herself. She removes her skis, heads off behind a tree, and pulls her pants down. She accidentally lets go of her skis, which start down the mountain. With her pants down around her ankles, she lunges forward to grab the skis. Not only does she miss them, she slips and starts sliding down the mountain on her bare backside. In this manner she goes all the way to the bottom.

Later she is in the emergency room of the local hospital having her scrapes and bruises attended to and a man comes in. The emergency room staff is surprised to see this man, as he is reputed to be the best skier on the mountain. It is obvious that he has dislocated his shoulder.

"How did you do that?" asked one of the nurses.

"Well, I was going up the lift and happened to look down and saw something go by that was so unbelievable that I pulled my shoulder out when I turned around to see if it was real."

"What was it?"

"If I told you, you wouldn't believe me."

The Strange Gas Station Attendant

A young woman must return home from college in the middle of the night because of a sudden illness in her family. Her nervousness increases after she pulls into a filling station because the attendant keeps looking at her in an odd manner. After he pumps the gas, he insists that she get out of the car. She resists, but he finally convinces her to get out and see because it could be a "major problem with the car." As she gets out, he grabs her, pushes her into the gas station office, and locks the door behind them. As she opens her mouth to scream, he says calmly, "I'm sorry I had to do that, but there's a man lying on the backseat of the car with a knife."

(In one version of this popular college tale, the coed and the man at the gas station fall in love and get married.)

THE TOASTED TANNER

Since the very invention of electricity, worrywarts have fretted about the ill effects of being around light bulbs, or battery-powered radios, or even refrigerators. When the first electric light bulbs were installed in 1879, public fears were so inflamed that signs were posted assuring people that "the use of electricity for lighting is in no way harmful to health, nor does it affect the soundness of sleep."*

The advent of radar during World War II gave a quantum boost to the fears of "electronic contamination"—and in some instances, with considerable justification. Now a new menace is afoot in the land that seems of especial danger to yuppies and other fitness freaks.

It is the deadly tanning salon.

Abigail Van Buren gave a typical account of the scare in her "Dear Abby" column of September 22, 1987, in *The Washington Times.* A woman reported receiving a letter from daughter Kathy, a student in Provo, Utah. The account was as follows: A seventeen-year-old girl won a trip to Hawaii and decided to go to a tanning parlor to get prepped for the trip. She was told that the limit was thirty minutes a day. Wanting a rush job, she visited seven parlors in one day, staying under the lamps for a total of three and a half hours.

She "microwaved herself . . . just cooked herself from the inside out!" The report put the girl in Utah Valley Regional Medical Center in Provo, blinded and with "about 26 days to live." The writer concluded, "You may want to verify these facts in Provo."

Ms. Van Buren attempted to do just that and predictably no such patient existed. A spokeswoman at the hospital said the story had been circulating among students at Brigham Young University and that it had also surfaced in Pocatello, Idaho.

As noted, this report was printed in 1987. Before that, hurry-up tanners had "microwaved themselves" in virtually every city in America that boasts of a tanning salon, and the ru-

*Paper by Admiral Hyman G. Rickover, quoted in *The Congressional Record,* Aug. 2, 1979, p. S 11527.

mor shows no signs of abating. The manager of a salon in Washington, D.C., tells us that he's received "perhaps a dozen calls in the last year" from news reporters checking reports of over-toasted tanners in his shop. "I tell them to check Burger King," he said.

THE SELF-COMBUSTING BODY

The City News Bureau in Chicago, a cooperative that supplies local news to the Chicago media, is run by hard-bitten editors who pride themselves on accuracy and ensuring that stories come from verifiable, trusted sources. "If your mother says she loves you," an old CNB saying goes, "check it out." Thus journalists gave reflexive credence to a story that moved over the bureau's wires in early August 1982: "A woman was killed Thursday as she was walking in the 4000 block of South Wells and for no known reason burst into flames, police said."

Later the bureau added that a possible cause of the incident might be "spontaneous human combustion." United Press International picked up the story, also implying that spontaneous human combustion caused the woman to go up in flames as she walked down the street in front of an eyewitness.

Reporter Tom Zito of *The Washington Post* wrote an account, "The Mysterious History of Spontaneous Combustion," on August 7, 1982, which noted that the fear is well supported in fiction if not in fact.

Herman Melville, in his novel *Redburn,* described a drunken sailor so soaked with rum that he self-ignited. "Two threads of greenish fire, like a forked tongue, darted out between the lips; and in a moment, the cadaverous face was crawled over by a swarm of worm-like flames."

Charles Dickens, in *Bleak House,* had a character named Krook who went up in self-combusted smoke. Krook's spectacles and pipe are found lying in front of his easy chair, in a room filled with smoke. Persons who read the manuscript challenged Dickens, who added a preface saying that he had given the subject serious study and found "about 30 cases on record" of spontaneous combustion that he found credible. He cited a French countess who disappeared into a heap of ashes by her bedside in 1731, only her legs remaining intact.

But the Cook County Medical Examiner, Dr. Robert Stein, said after the autopsy that the Chicago woman was dead before she burned, and that the crime lab found traces of hydrocarbon accelerants on her clothing. "There's no such thing as spontaneous combustion here," he said. The City News Bureau at that point said it was reporting only what it was told by the police.

The skeptical Associated Press never used the story because managing editor Wick Temple relied upon common sense rather than what a beat cop told a reporter: "Since the human body is 98 percent water, I had a hard time believing it."

THE KIDNEY-SNATCHING SURGEON

In the spring of 1991 alarmed New Yorkers began asking why the media were "covering up" reports about a surgeon who was snatching people off the street and removing organs for sale to transplant patients. Reporter Patrice O'Shaughnessy of the *New York Daily News* wrote on April 30, 1991, that her newspaper and the police received frantic phone calls relating several versions of the story:

• *"A guy gets drunk, wanders into the wrong apartment, wakes up the next day with stitches and finds out that a kidney is gone."*

• *"Two out-of-town, inebriated businessmen meet a beautiful woman in a Manhattan bar. One of them leaves with her. The next day, after a mysterious telephone message, the other businessman finds his friend taped to a bed in a Bowery hotel. He has an intravenous tube in his arm and a surgical incision. His kidney had been removed."*

• *"A blond woman or transvestite serial killer is running rampant in midtown, murdering young men and stealing their organs. Their hearts and livers were taken . . . and the incisions were perfect—like a surgeon's."*

• *"The mob is sponsoring the body-snatching to fuel a black market in kidneys . . ."*

Reporter O'Shaughnessy had to look no further than her *TV Guide* to discover the source of the Mad Kidney-Snatcher stories. On April 2 the popular NBC-TV show "Law and Order" had a segment about a man getting mugged in Central Park and waking up to discover that someone had removed one of his kidneys. But was the incident based on fact or imagination? The show's writer, Joe Morgenstern, said that the idea came from someone who had heard of a newspaper article about such an incident—yet he never actually saw the article, nor could he find anyone who had. Morgenstern told reporters he actually began hearing the story repeated back to him as gospel before the "Law and Order" episode even aired, thanks to "an overtalkative crew during filming in New York."

The story quickly leaped to Washington, where a *Washington Post* editor heard it recounted at a dinner party, attributed to a "daughter in New York, who heard it recently from a school friend, who heard it from someone who actually knew the principals."

Reporter Lloyd Grove spent several days trying to track down the story. He could not, but he picked up a "similar tale from the lady at the telefax shop, who heard it from a girlfriend, who heard it from a cousin, who heard it from a worker."

Oddly, the story might have started in Moscow, in the directorate of the old KGB that was responsible for stirring up nasty rumors about Uncle Sam. Herbert Romerstein, a disinformation specialist for the United States Information Agency, published a study in 1987 of rumors rampant in Latin America that doctors were "buying babies" whose organs would be transplanted into "rich Americans." Romerstein traced the original article to a Central American newspaper that the Soviets often used as a conduit through which they launched anti-American rumors. Once the article is printed, regardless of the credibility of the publication, it can then be fed to other media who cite a named source for the information.

As recently as April 18, 1993, a Renta story from Teguciagalpa, Honduras, repeated rumors and denials, alleging that Honduran children were being kidnapped for the purpose of selling their organs. Not all the papers carrying the story bothered to carry the denials in their versions.

AIDS WARNING ON THE MIRROR

A similar story swept yuppiedom at about the same time, once again with John Barleycorn and Eros as central characters. A young man meets a beautiful woman in a bar and they end up in his apartment in bed. He awakes the next morning to find that she has left a message scrawled in lipstick across his bathroom mirror: "Welcome to the World of AIDS!" The woman supposedly was infected with AIDS during a casual affair and is reaping revenge by spreading the disease to as many men as she can seduce. *(Just how this motive becomes known to the victim is somewhat fuzzy.)*

In any event, the story has cropped up as far away as a resort in western Jamaica, where the son of one of the authors was assured in the winter of 1992 that it happened "just down the beach, at that other club," only a day or two earlier. Having already heard the story at several of Washington's most reputable saloons, he was properly dubious.

BLUSHING IN THE BUFF

Apparently many American women do their housework in the nude, but nervously so, given the number of persons who knock on the door during any given day. When living in a Philadelphia suburb one of the authors heard an account of what happened to "Mary, who lives down the street." During a day of naked housecleaning "Mary" decided to fix a leaky drain in a laundry tub in the basement. Water kept dripping onto her head, so she picked up her son's football helmet and put it on. She was crouched on the floor under the tub, wrench in hand and stark naked (save for the helmet) when the gas meter reader suddenly came in through the unlocked basement door. They stared at one another a long moment, then the meter reader said, "Lady, I don't know what position you play, but I sure as hell wish I could see your team's next game."

Years later the author summoned enough courage to ask "Mary" if the story was in fact true. She giggled and said, "It happened, but not to me; the lady was someone who knew one of my sister's friends who lived in Pittsburgh. Or was it Detroit?"

No, in Ohio, according to a reader quoted in an Ann Landers column in *The Washington Post* on December 17, 1992. The reader asked if Landers "happened to see the item in the paper about the Ohio housewife who was doing her laundry in the basement . . ." You know the rest of the story. In this instance, the meter reader's punch line was: "I hope your team wins, lady."

A variant popular in Great Britain is the nude housecleaner who hears a knock on the door and the call, "Blind man." Feeling charitable, she opens the door (in the buff) to hand the beggar some money. He is holding a large, long package. He looks at her oddly and says, "Here are the new Venetian blinds your husband ordered. Where do you want them?"

Ann Landers has carried on an amusing exchange of what she calls "Lady Godiva" stories with readers. In 1986 she supervised a brisk debate among readers on the question of whether women are "exhibitionists" if they work around the house naked. A woman who signed herself "Still Blushing" said that a "recent experience cured me" of the habit. Landers gave her account in a column in *The Washington Post* on May 19, 1986:

The woman was doing housework naked when her minister telephoned to say he wished to drop by to see her new baby. She discovered that she was out of coffee cream and telephoned a woman neighbor to ask if she could bring a cup. "I'll be there in a few minutes," the neighbor said. The woman, still nude, was rushing around to tidy up the house when the doorbell rang. She wrapped a small towel around her midriff and opened the door and shouted, "Boy, am I glad to see you, honey!"

The minister mumbled, "I'll be back next week when I can bring my wife."

THE ELEPHANT AND THE CAR

The late Hughes Rudd had a funny story for listeners on the CBS Radio Network in the spring of 1976. A woman "somewhere in the South" attended a circus and returned to the parking lot to find the front of her Volkswagen smashed. An apologetic circus official told her that a trainer had been exercising an elephant in the parking lot as the music began. The elephant "began its act" and, lacking the normal props, perched on the front of the car. The woman was able to drive away because the VW has its engine in the back. But her troubles didn't end at the circus: friends and relatives guffawed in disbelief when she explained what had happened, accusing her of making up a wild story as an excuse for sloppy driving.

As recounted by columnist Gloria Borger in the Washington *Star* on May 26, 1978, an elephant had done the same thing in Milwaukee a decade earlier, and a local reporter called Hughes Rudd to task for spreading a "myth." He wrote: "Where is it that old elephants go to die? If you find out, let us know so that we can send old elephant stories there to perish, too."

One place the "old elephants" go is to game parks in Great Britain, where folklorists report hearing variants of the elephant/car story.

"SAVE A MILLION BOTTLE CAPS . . ."

A story that repeatedly bedevils officials of health organizations goes as follows: collect X-number of cigarette packages, or soft drink bottle caps, and trade them in so that a kidney patient can receive free time on a dialysis machine, or a little girl can get free open-heart surgery, or a blind man will be given a seeing-eye dog. Bob Levey, writer of a popular local column in *The Washington Post,* debunks such yarns about once a year— with frustration dripping from his words. He wrote on November 26, 1982:

"I'm no public opinion pollster, but I do have a rule of thumb. One phone call in a week about a subject makes it 'of interest.' Two calls make it a 'possible trend.' Three make it a 'definite trend.' Four make it a 'surge.' It has been surging lately—about one of the oldest, falsest stories ever to do the rounds."

Then Levey recounted the "dialysis machine" rumors, and the difficulty he had in convincing inquirers that the story was a won't-go-away myth. One woman told Levey she had two footlockers filled with empty Lucky Strike packages. He told her to throw them in the trash, that they were worthless. "Oh, I couldn't do that," she said. "Kidney disease runs in my family, and you just never know when you might need them."

Levey wrote about the hoax again on April 15, 1985, and an official of the National Kidney Foundation listed for him the items that gullible persons had been stashing: cigarette packs, the silver paper from cigarette packs, lift-top tabs from soda cans, coupons from Betty Crocker or other manufacturers, Universal Product Codes of different items, used postage stamps, grocery store receipts, and grocery store bags. None of these items, in whatever quantity, buys a single minute of dialysis, the official said, nor has the kidney foundation ever sponsored such a program.

"Let's hope that settles it," Levey wrote. "I suspect it won't, but it's spring, and hope springs eternal."

THE DOBERMAN AND THE FINGERS

Dewey Webb, who writes for *New Times,* a tabloid published in Phoenix, Arizona, had an archetypal series of sources when he began running down the southwestern version of this story: someone in an industrial plant who heard it from another employee who heard it from a credit union clerk who swore that it happened to either her sister or her cousin (the initial informant couldn't remember which) who lived in Las Vegas. In any event, here is what supposedly happened, as Webb wrote in the *New Times* for March 2–8, 1983:

A woman returned from work to find her dog lying on the floor, gasping for breath. She rushed him to the vet, who immediately said, "Tracheotomy," and told her to leave the pet overnight. She had no sooner returned home when the vet phoned and said, "Get out of the house immediately. Go next door to the neighbor's and call the police." The vet sounded so alarmed that the woman did as directed without asking any questions.

The vet, when he began operating, found two human fingers lodged in the dog's throat. The police, upon searching the house, found an intruder hidden in the closet, two fingers missing from his hand, bleeding to death.

Reporter Webb called the *Las Vegas Sun* to see what coverage the story had been given. The city editor (predictably) laughed and said the story had been going around Las Vegas for weeks, and that the police said no such thing had happened. In their city, anyway. But one cop had been talking to a friend out in Los Angeles, and this guy had heard of a fellow who . . .

Through the 1980s the oft-repeated yarn usually featured a Doberman, the watchdog of choice of the decade. Versions heard around the Washington, D.C., area during the early 1990s replaced the Doberman with a pit bull, a breed that got wide (and seemingly deserved) publicity for being a bad actor.

A variant heard around Front Royal, Virginia, during the 1970s was of a farmer who had a finger cut off in an accident with a tractor. He was rushed to the hospital, where the doctor said the finger could be restored if sewn on quickly enough. The farmer's brother rushed back to the tractor—and found the family dog finishing a snack of the finger.

But who was the hapless victim? No one ever could produce any firmer identification than "some fellow who lives down in Page County."

TURKEY NECK TRAUMA

This one is rather grisly, so if you are squeamish, move on to the next heading.

OK, we warned you. A man goes out drinking on Thanksgiving Day, comes home tipsy, and falls asleep on the sofa, the fly of his trousers open. His teenaged sons come in a while later and decide to play a prank on Dad. They get a turkey neck out of the refrigerator and leave it dangling from his fly and go upstairs for the night.

At first light, Mom comes downstairs to find the family cat noisily munching on the turkey neck protruding from her husband's fly. She faints.

No griping; we warned you.

STUCK WITH THE CHECK

During the 1950s one of the authors frequently hitchhiked to and from the University of Texas. A businessman who gave him a ride passed on a warning about a scam to which he claimed to have fallen victim during his own hitchhiking days. A driver offered to buy him dinner, and they stopped at a rather expensive roadside restaurant. After they finished, the driver said, "You go ahead and enjoy another cup of coffee, I'm going to have the tank filled with gas so we won't have to stop again. You wave back when I get to the cashier's so that he'll know that you're with me." The hitchhiker waved as directed, finished his coffee, fretted when the driver didn't return in fifteen minutes or so, and finally decided he'd go on outside. The cashier stopped him at the door. "Hey," he said, "you haven't paid the bill." The hitchhiker told him that the other man was going to pay. "That's not what he told me," the cashier said. "He said you would take care of the check, and that you would wave to me to confirm it."

Sure enough, the driver and his car were gone when the cashier and the hitchhiker went outside. The restaurant owner eventually accepted the hitchhiker's story but only after a long wrangle.

With hitchhiking now more or less passé, folklorist Jan Harold Brunvand reports (in *Curses! Broiled Again!*) that the scam has moved indoors, to the grocery store. An old lady stops another shopper and insists that he is the image of her dead son.

He graciously permits her to push her cart through the checkout line ahead of him, and then agrees to trot off in search of something (a can of peas or another loaf of bread) that she has forgotten. "Thank you, dear son," she says loud enough to be overheard by the cashier. When the man returns, the woman and her groceries are gone. And, of course, "Mother" has left her bill with the cashier for her "dear son" to pay.

THE FLYING CAT

Any story repeated often enough to be the subject of a call to a newspaper column warrants Urban Myth status, so again we go to the resources of Bob Levey of *The Washington Post,* in a column published June 1, 1987. The story came from "a woman who heard it from her hairdresser." Levey wrote of the couple who took in a stray kitten. The cat, for reasons known only to cats, climbed up a birch tree in the backyard and refused to come down, regardless of pleas and offers of food. The husband looped a rope over the branch and tried to pull the kitty down within reach, whereupon the rope broke, the branch snapped back, and the kitten sailed over the fence and out of sight. The couple was unable to find it.

A week or so later they encountered a neighbor at the grocery store. He was buying a bag of cat food. "We didn't know you had a cat," they said.

"I didn't until last week. But Joe and I were sitting out on the patio the other day when this kitten dropped out of the sky, just like that. Fell right into Joe's lap."

(Query: Just how far was this kitten supposed to have flown? If the original "owners" made even a perfunctory search, would not they have encountered the couple looking for the launch pad of the flying feline? Levey of the Post *could find no one actually involved in the incident, although several persons insisted they had "heard" it happened in the Cleveland Park section of Washington.)*

THE CHURCH BROADCAST BAN

For almost two decades the Federal Communications Commission, the federal agency that regulates the broadcast industry, has been deluged with protests about a supposed new regulation that would ban the broadcast of Sunday worship services in churches. The impetus for the "rule" supposedly came from the prominent atheist Madalyn Murray O'Hair, who played a role in the legal action that led to the U.S. Supreme Court's 1963 ban on prayers in public schools.

According to the FCC press office, no less than 21 million pieces of mail have been received on the "worship ban" in the last fifteen years. The FCC replies with a printed "fact sheet" stating that no such rule is under consideration.

Despite the FCC's widely publicized denials over the years, the mail keeps coming. Bill Simmons of the Associated Press reported a typical rebirth of the rumor from Little Rock, Arkansas, in December 1992. A man visited several area churches distributing a one-page "important notice" alerting members to the supposed FCC proceeding. The flier claimed that if the O'Hair petition succeeded, "all Sunday worship services being broadcast, either by radio or television, will stop." O'Hair has repeatedly told news organizations she is involved in no such campaign.

According to the FCC, a petition was filed in 1974—but not by O'Hair—asking for an investigation of noncommercial educational broadcast stations, including those that are licensed to religious groups. But in a 1975 announcement the FCC declined to investigate, saying that the First Amendment to the U.S. Constitution requires it to be neutral on religion. But the proceeding prompted the first of what became a tidal wave of protests about the "ban." Technology has now increased the flow: the FCC says that it receives faxes almost daily from concerned citizens, as well as letters and postcards.

A Toolbox of Trouble

A recurring favorite in New York City concerns the little old lady whose beloved cat dies. Rather than toss Tabby into the trash, she wraps the corpse in a neat package and boards a subway for Queens, seeking a quiet park where she can give her pet a decent burial. En route, of course, a thief snatches away her package and flees. You are required to use your imagination about the thief's reaction when he inspects his booty.

In another version, the little old lady decides to wrap the dead cat in brown paper and take it downtown, where she can leave it so that someone else can worry about burial. She first tries to leave it on the bus, but this doesn't work, for another passenger notices and runs after her to give her the package. This is repeated all day, as the woman leaves the package on the corner, in coffee shops, on another bus. Defeated, she returns home and decides to open the package and take a last look at her beloved tabby. She unties the package and finds a leg of lamb.

A variation concerns the man who lives in the suburbs and works in the city, and who wishes to fertilize a struggling side-walk tree near his office. On the weekend he goes to a stable and collects five or so pounds of horse manure, which he bundles into a sack so he can take it into town on Monday. Again, a snatch-and-run thief on the subway—hopefully the same sneak who is still trying to figure out what to do with that dead cat.

Michael Stackpole, the esteemed science fiction writer from Phoenix, Arizona, chortles as he passes along a Western version, which he testifies is gospel true: "In an observatory in Tucson, workers arriving early one morning discovered a wild-cat had gotten inside the building. They trapped it eventually and ended up putting it in a big toolbox owned by a guy who had not yet showed up at work. When he arrived, his colleagues told him what they had done, and after almost getting his nose taken off by an angry cat, he agreed to take the beast out into the local woods and release him.

"He put his toolbox in the back of his pickup, then returned inside for his coat. As he came back out he saw a car speeding away and, of course, the toolbox was gone! The man followed the car and, coming over a rise, saw it in a ditch beside the road, with four very shaken young men standing near it. They had opened the box to see what sort of prize they'd taken and 'ROAR' they developed a problem."

THE AX MAN COMETH

In 1983 columnist Elaine Viets of the *St. Louis Post-Dispatch* began hearing about a bizarre episode that informants said happened at the St. Clair Square shopping mall.

Or perhaps Chesterfield Mall. Well, Mays Center, perhaps? Or was it South County? In any event, after arduous work on the telephone she began her account on June 1, 1983, this way: "Warning: The following story is not true. I repeat: It is not true. Even if you know someone who works with the sister of the woman it happened to." Ms. Viets related a typical version:

"This young girl was shopping at Chesterfield Mall, and she came out to her car. Sitting inside was an old woman. The girl said, 'Pardon me, ma'am, you're in the wrong car.'

" 'I'm so tired,' the old lady says. 'I had to sit down.'

"The girl feels sorry for her. The old lady wants a ride home. The girl is about to take her when she remembers her car was locked. Quickly, she makes up an excuse. 'My sister's still shopping inside. I'll go get her and we'll take you home.'

"Instead, the girl goes inside and comes back with mall security. There's a scuffle. The old lady's gray wig is knocked off. She's really a man. Under the car seat they find an ax."

In some of the accounts ("a man who got it from the woman who works with his wife") the Ax Man sees the cops coming and runs into the woods, or drives away in the car, or is caught running across the parking lot by uniformed police.

Believers are undeterred by the fact that the story does not make the newspapers. "Powerful retailers bribed the police and reporters to keep silent," Ms. Viets wrote. (Oddly, one of the "sources" she ran across was an ad salesman for her own *Post-Dispatch*.) A St. Louis policeman told Ms. Viets that he heard about the Ax Man "from someone who works with my sister. I checked with homicide. They heard it happened in Vegas."

Ms. Viets discovered that shopping-mall myths are a recurring phenomenon. "Last time, a young boy was supposed to have been castrated in a washroom at Northwood Plaza, St. Clair Square, etc. Two years before that, the centers were supposed to be infested with lice. Two years ago, the Ax Man cometh."

The Ax Man story is a variant of what Jan Harold Brunvand has called the "Hairy Armed Hitchhiker." A young woman picks up an older woman hitchhiker who claims she has missed her bus. As they chat, the younger woman notices that her passenger has hairy, muscular arms. She stops the car on a pretext and calls the cops, who discover that the "other woman" is in fact a man—perhaps even an escaped killer—who has an ax in his handbag.

Brunvand feels such stories arise from the warnings given

about checking the back of your car before you get in and being careful about giving help to strangers.

The Surprise Party

We've heard this story told, variously, about a former star performer for the Washington Redskins, an editor of the old Washington *Star,* an assistant secretary of state, and a couple of businessmen; printed versions elsewhere have mentioned professors and executives. But the core story goes this way:

An executive is miffed the morning of his fortieth birthday when neither his wife nor his three children offer a word of congratulations. He goes to the office and gripes to his secretary about the lack of familial attention. "You poor fellow," she says, "let me take you to lunch. I'll show you that someone cares for you."

They have a splendid respite, and martinis and wine flow in profusion. Then the secretary suggests, "It's already after three o'clock. Why don't we take the rest of the afternoon off and go to my apartment and relax?" The man eagerly agrees. When they arrive, the secretary says, "Make yourself at home while I go slip into something more comfortable," and leaves the room.

Aha! the man thinks; after years of lusting for this woman I am about to succeed. He strips off his clothes and stands in the middle of the room, awaiting her return.

The door opens. "Surprise!" someone yells. His wife walks in carrying a birthday cake, forty candles ablaze, followed by his three children, his mother-in-law, the secretary, the entire office staff, his neighbors. . . .

A Thief's Apology

A couple's car is stolen from the driveway. Several days later it reappears with a note on the windshield: "Please pardon our unforgivable behavior in taking your car. A sudden emergency arose which made it essential for us to have transportation. The story is too involved to explain, and we are also too embarrassed to talk to you in person. As a token of our regret, would you please be our guests at the theater later this week?" Enclosed are two prime tickets for a Broadway show.

When the couple returns home from the theater they find that their entire house has been ransacked.

THE EXPLODING ISRAELI COCKROACH

In August 1988 the *Jerusalem Post* reported on an Israeli woman who caught a cockroach and threw it into the commode. Unable to watch the insect drown, she squirted it with a pesticide. Her husband came home a bit later, sat down on the john, and dropped a cigarette into the bowl. BOOM! There was substantial fire damage to his bottom and other exposed parts. An ambulance crew was summoned to take him to the hospital. Attendants asked what had happened; when they heard the story they laughed so hard they dropped the stretcher, breaking the fellow's arm.

A woman announcer who read this item over WTOP Radio in Washington on the afternoon of August 25, 1988, laughed so hard she was unintelligible. So, too, was Allan Christian of WFBR in Baltimore the next afternoon. One of the authors who heard this radio report and read the item in print was not surprised at a one-paragraph item in *The Washington Times* on September 1, 1988:

JERUSALEM—The *Jerusalem Post* retracted yesterday an amusing report carried on this page last Friday about a housewife's battle with a cockroach that landed her husband in the hospital, saying it could not substantiate the story.

We were not surprised; see pages 152–53 for the domestic generic equivalent of the Israeli yarn.

DEPARTMENT STORE HORRORS

Major retailers in virtually every American city have been the subject of false reports of Awful Happenings on their premises—of spiders or Oriental tarantulas lurking in potted plants; of viper fangs concealed in the lining of parkas, waiting to poison the buyer; of bathing suits that become transparent when wet.

The veteran Washington newspaperman Jerry O'Leary writes of a story he heard while working for the old Washington *Star.* "A Washington department store in the mid-1930s was damaged mightily when a rumor spread that a dress had been returned by a customer after having been used to drape a corpse at a funeral. The false tale had it that the dress was resold and caused dreadful illness to the second buyer because of the residue of formaldehyde," O'Leary wrote in *The Washington Times* on June 2, 1989, in a discussion of Washington rumors.

Martin F. Kohn of the *Detroit Free Press* expended vast journalistic energy in 1981 trying to run down a story that he related as follows (on October 21, 1981):

A woman shopping at a K Mart store in Troy tries on a coat. As she puts one of her arms through the sleeve, she feels a sting like a pinprick. She thinks nothing of it until she gets home and her arm begins to swell up. She is rushed to William Beaumont Hospital in Royal Oak, where her arm is amputated in order to save her life.

The coat, it seems, was made in Taiwan, and somehow a poisonous snake had laid its eggs in the carton of coats. The eggs hatched in the lining and one of the baby snakes bit the woman.

According to reporter Kohn, at least half a dozen versions of the story circulated in Detroit, with both the locale and the outcome shifting (in one version, the woman died). He wrote: "The version here was told to a reporter by a friend who is a trustworthy bank executive. She in turn heard it from a coworker whose mother is a trustworthy nurse at Beaumont Hospital. The nurse heard it one night from three different hospital employees, who all said they heard it second-hand."

Urban myth guru Jan Harold Brunvand told the *Detroit Free Press* that he first began hearing this story in the late 1960s, at the height of American involvement in Vietnam. He told Kohn, "It may be a subconscious metaphor about our guilt in Vietnam, that we're getting back [from the Far East] what we deserve." The first printed version he found was in the *Buffalo Evening News* in 1969.

Why He Wouldn't Say "Bow Wow"

Writer Gary Meece, reviewing an earlier version of this book for the esteemed *Memphis Commercial Appeal* on March 27, 1983, offered "an example of an urban folk tale" that might show up "in some future edition." You're right, Gary, and thanks for your contribution to urban mythology:

A woman who lives in Manhattan vacationed recently in Acapulco. One afternoon, as she was walking along the beach, she noticed that she was being followed by what was apparently a small lost dog.

It followed her back to the hotel. Since it seemed friendly enough, she let it into her room and fed it. Over the next few days she grew more attached to her new pet. When it came time to return to New York, she smuggled the Chihuahua-sized animal home in her luggage.

She pampered and loved her new pet and it seemed to thrive for a while, but one day it became ill. When she took it in for treatment the veterinarian was out, so she left it overnight.

The next morning, the veterinarian called and asked excitedly, "Where did you get that animal?"

Disturbed by his manner, she admitted she had smuggled her little dog into the United States.

"That's no dog, that's a rat," replied the vet.

(You will note that reporter Meece made the butt of his story a Yankee, for as every Southern newspaperman knows, no one from Manhattan has enough common sense to figure out how to shell a peanut.)

Six Plus Six Plus Six Equals Satan?

As is well known to every diabolist, the numbers 666 symbolize the Antichrist beast, per the Book of Revelation: "Let him that hath understanding count the number of the beast . . . and his number is Six hundred threescore and six." Thus the Reverend Robert McCurry of Calvary Temple in East Point,

Georgia, exuded alarm in the early 1980s when he discovered the Internal Revenue Service used "666" as the number of its form for retirement plans.

Soon the pastor blanketed the South—well, part of it, anyway—with leaflets warning of the subtlety of Satan and that through his efforts the federal government was making society the "kingdom of the Antichrist."

Protests by McCurry and other alert Satan-watchers hit Washington with such force that the IRS announced it would no longer use "666" as the number for the form.

The New York Times, in reporting this victory for anti-Satanists in an editorial on September 28, 1982, noted some other places where the dread figures might appear; telephone exchanges, credit cards, department store charge accounts, Social Security cards, driver's licenses, cash machine identity codes, "not to mention the Manhattan penthouse restaurant Top of the Sixes, which is located at an insinuating address, 666 Fifth Avenue."

At about the same time, *The Wall Street Journal* alerted readers about graffiti being sprayed around Washington: "666 Reagan Devil." Apparently someone had counted the number of letters in R-o-n-a-l-d W-i-l-s-o-n R-e-a-g-a-n.

THE RADIATED SAILORS

For years the U.S. Navy dealt with persistent—and false—rumors that radiation-induced cancer killed the crew of the first nuclear-powered submarine, the *Nautilus*. In frustration the navy in 1978 finally tracked down each of the ninety-six officers and enlisted men of the first crew. "Despite the rumors," Admiral Hyman Rickover said in the 1979 speech cited earlier, "all the men associated with operating the nuclear propulsion plant were alive and well."

UNSAFE BATTLEFIELD SEX

A story popular with Civil War buffs concerns the Southern lass who became pregnant without benefit of intercourse. According to a Tennessee woman who wrote Abigail Van Buren

(*The Washington Times,* November 6, 1987), the curious event occurred May 12, 1863, in this fashion: "A young Virginia farm girl was standing on her front porch when a stray bullet first passed through the scrotum of a young Union cavalryman, then lodged in the reproductive tract of the young woman, who thus became pregnant by a man she had not been within 100 feet of! And nine months later she gave birth to a healthy baby."

Ms. Van Buren reported hearing the same story about an Indian maiden who claimed she was impregnated by a bow and arrow. "Maybe that's where the traditional Indian greeting 'How?' originated," she commented.

THE LSD TATTOO PAPER

In the autumn of 1988 a horrifying story swept across New Jersey, alarming parents, school officials, and law enforcement officers. Drug dealers were distributing tiny pieces of "tattoo paper" in the form of blue stars or cartoon characters which were intended for use by children. But the "tattoos" had been soaked in the hallucinatory drug LSD. Children were said to buy the tattoo stickers and put them in their mouths or on their skin and immediately begin to hallucinate. In some instances, persons stuck the tattoo papers on unsuspecting kids.

The rumor was given impetus by a widely circulated leaflet headed, PUBLIC SERVICE ANNOUNCEMENT, which read as follows:

A form of tatoo [sic] called "BLUE STAR" is being sold to school children. It is a small sheet of white paper containing a blue star, the size of a pencil eraser. Each star is soaked with LSD.

Each star can be removed and placed in the mouth. THE LSD CAN ALSO BE ABSORBED THROUGH THE SKIN BY HANDLING THE PAPER.

There is also [sic] brightly colored tabs resembling postage stamps that have pictures of Superman, butterflies, clowns, Mickey Mouse and other Disney characters on them.

These stamps are packed in a red cardboard box wrapped in foil.

This is a new way of selling ACID by appealing to young children. A child could happen upon these and have a fatal "trip."

The leaflet concluded by urging parents or teachers who saw the tattoo papers to call the police. "Please feel free to reproduce this article and distribute it to your staff, or within your community. FOR THOSE OF YOU WITH SMALL CHILDREN, THIS IS VERY SCARY INFORMATION BUT IMPORTANT FOR YOU TO KNOW." The leaflet was signed "Sheriff Edward J. Weister, Union City Police Department."

Reporter Gina Kolata chased this story across the Jersey moors for *The New York Times* and found that it had visited towns up and down the state. Not surprisingly, she wrote on December 9, 1988, no child had been found who actually used any tattoo-LSD. "Sheriff Weister" proved nonexistent, although the flier bearing his name circulated by the uncountable thousands. An official of the Federal Drug Enforcement Administration told Ms. Kolata, "It's a very poor practical joke," and added it was doubtful that enough LSD could be put on a sticker to have any effects.

The ever-vigilant Jan Harold Brunvand immediately reported to *The New York Times,* via a letter published December 24, 1988, that English folklorists Iona and Peter Opie had traced a similar story to 1840, when gummed postage stamps called "penny blacks" or "Queen's heads" were introduced into the British mails. The glue was alleged to be poisonous, and that "those so rash as to lick the Queen's head were in danger of contacting cholera."

Similar tattoo-LSD rumors were reported as far away as Alaska, where reporters for the *Anchorage Daily News* and KTVF-TV did ain't-so stories in November 1988, and even in Lima, Peru, where a Spanish version of the warning leaflet appeared on a bulletin board at the United States Embassy and Agency for International Development. Another *New York Times* reader wrote that during a tour of the FBI Building in Washington in August 1988, "we were informed by our tour guide that LSD-laced tattoos were a new threat and that we should warn our children." And yet another reader who professed a knowledge of drugs stated that "modern chemistry has refined the manufacture of LSD to the point where a speck of dust the size of a pinpoint can contain 400 micrograms of the chemical"—four times the normal dosage "recommended" by LSD pioneer Timothy Leary in his book *The Psychedelic Experience.*

This reader warned about the dangers of being ignorant of drugs. He wrote: "Recently, a highway patrolman put his finger into and tasted what he thought was a citizen's cocaine. He knew what cocaine tasted like and that doing so would not produce its effects. Learning that the substance was not cocaine, he let the driver go. Unfortunately, the patrolman did not know that crystal LSD can look very much like cocaine and that its effects are not immediate. He is still in the hospital, while an obvious LSD offender is at large." Oddly, the reader's account was strikingly void of the time/place/name details that would take the story out of the Urban Myth mold.

Baby Boomer

Here's a favorite that comes out of hospitals with astounding frequency: a baby is hooked up to a respirator but by accident is given an "adult dose" of some kind of gas. The baby explodes. The hospital manages to persuade the local police department to cover up the death, but a concerned citizen calls the local newspaper.

Such is what happened at the Prince Georges's *County Journal* in suburban Washington in the autumn of 1986. Reporters there could find no trace of the exploding baby. Matt Neufeld of *The Washington Times* tried his hand as well, but had to inform readers on October 1, 1986, that the cops guffawed when he called for information—that the story is one of those yarns that are the bane of desk sergeants and newspapermen.

In the process, however, Neufeld learned about "The Missing Squad Car," a staple of Washington-area police mythology. It seems that a police officer pulls over a drunken driver in Fairfax County, Virginia. A tow truck is called. As the drunk's car is being hooked up to the tow truck, he suddenly jumps into the officer's police car and speeds away, lights flashing. The car is found several days later in someone else's driveway. Or in a barn.

Or on an overlook on the George Washington Parkway. Or . . . you get the idea.

Leave My Cookies Alone!

On January 26, 1990, Jerry O'Leary of *The Washington Times,* one of the city's most experienced and respected newsmen, wrote a column concerning a story he had heard about an Air Force second lieutenant named Mitchell W. Clapp, which went this way:

Clapp was on a plane trip and had to spend two hours in the St. Louis airport between flights. He bought a cup of coffee and a package of Oreo cookies and found a seat at a table with a Marine Corps brigadier general described as a "mean-looking man with hair, an honest-to-God scar on his forehead, and six rows of ribbons including the Silver Star." Clapp satisfied protocol with a nod and "Good Morning, sir!" and turned to the crossword puzzle, whereupon he heard the unmistakable sound of crinkling cellophane. He glanced up and saw that the general had opened a package of Oreos and was eating one of them. Irked at the uninvited taking of his Oreos, and eager to show that he couldn't be cowed, Clapp reached into the package and took a cookie for himself.

Silence from the general, and no eye contact, although Clapp could see his expressionless face. Then the general took yet another cookie, and this time licked the creamy center out of it before "crunching the rest of it in his bulldog jaws." So Clapp grabbed another cookie for himself. He and the general alternated eating Oreos until the package was empty.

"When the lieutenant ate the last cookie," O'Leary wrote, "the public address system blared an announcement and the general rose to his feet, picked up the empty wrapper, threw it into the trash container, brushed the crumbs neatly off the table, and stalked away in a military manner."

Still marveling at the gall of the general, and feeling slightly foolish, Clapp picked up the rest of his paper—and found his unopened package of Oreos.

Segue to May 21, 1990—five months after the O'Leary column—and consider an interview in *The National Law Journal* with Chief Justice Alexander M. Sanders, Jr., of the South Carolina Court of Appeals. He was sitting in a shopping mall, eating peanut butter crackers and sipping a Coke, when a black man sat down at the table. Sanders was busy with his paper (as was the aforementioned Lieutenant Clapp) when the black man reached over and took a cracker.

Now, exactly what is the proper response to that? How big a deal is it? What are you supposed to do? What are you supposed to say? I chose not to say anything. I just looked at him. He just looked at me. I reached over and got a cracker and ate it. He reached over and got a cracker and ate it. By now, I am glaring at him. He is glaring at me. There is one cracker left. Our eyes are locked. He looks down first—he proverbially "blinks"—and pushes the last cracker over to me. I take the cracker, never taking my eyes off him, and eat it.

He gets up and leaves.

I pick up my paper. And there—under the paper—are my crackers. I was eating his crackers!

Interviewer John Monk tactfully noted that Judge Sanders calls some of his stories "urban myths." Monk continued, "When asked whether they are true, he dodges the question by saying, 'Some myths are true, but that's not the point, is it?' "

SPECIAL APPENDIX I: MENCKEN'S X-RATED CREDOS

When Mencken and Nathan finished *The American Credo* they put together a private collection of credos that were presumably too outrageous to appear in a book in 1920. The authors had their blue appendix privately published and distributed it to friends as a Christmas gift. Thanks to the Mencken Room at the Enoch Pratt Free Library in Baltimore, we have obtained a copy of the Christmas appendix. A sampling:

◆ That all floozies wear red neckties and colored handkerchiefs.

◆ That the couch in a theatrical manager's office is used at least twenty times a day.

◆ That toilet paper is quite unknown in the country, and all yokels use corncobs instead.

◆ That if a city man with a fresh shoeshine walks across a meadow he invariably steps into several large cowflops.

◆ That piles are caused by sitting on cold stone steps.

◆ That all United States senators have difficulty passing their water.

◆ That whenever the Elks hold a convention the whoremadams of the town bring in extra talent from five hundred miles around.

♦ That the dashboard of a country bean's buggy always bears the marks of his footprints upside down.

♦ That whenever a woman guest, fashionably dressed, takes the baby of the house in her lap, the baby pees.

SPECIAL APPENDIX II: A CHECKLIST FOR CRITICS

H. L. Mencken was perhaps one of the few serious writers who delighted in reading savage reviews of their work, and the more biting the commentary, the more he howled with glee. (Indeed, Mencken even published a short compilation of the more picturesque billingsgate directed at him in print, *Menckeniana: A Schimpflexikon,* Alfred A. Knopf, 1927.) Mencken carefully (perhaps even joyfully) clipped reviews of *The American Credo* and pasted them into his scrapbooks, which now adorn the Mencken Room of the Enoch Pratt Free Library in Baltimore. A sampling of what critics wrote of this predecessor volume to our own modest work:

The linguistic coat is brilliant and vari-colored, but this observation leads one on a converging trail of natural history. There is an animal of brilliant coat classified as an American *mephitine musteloid carnivore,* whose glands secrete a liquid of very offensive odor which can be ejected at will. But this animal doesn't trail in pairs, as a rule, and it doesn't become offensive unless some intruder crowds it.

—*The Dallas Morning News*

The writers apparently would have had as much fun at their volumes as would a couple of naughty children who stand up and ask awkward questions in Sunday school, but apparently they got so "het-up" that they became absolutely serious, which is always unfortunate for a critic. He then is apt to be both carried away and "put away" by those he criticizes.

—The Philadelphia *North American*

Little that is sacred to Americans escapes. Basing argument upon assertion that the man who is moral can never be honest, that morality and honesty have nothing in common, the authors ... spew right and left at laws, courts, institutions, authorities, professors, judges, uplifters, reformers ...

—*The News and Courier* (Charleston, S.C.)

It has been written with brains. It is a calm, careful, cautious, ably drawn, full-length portrait of America in all her boobery.... Rare as such an outcome may seem, there is some possibility that it may set someone thinking....

—*The Baltimore Sun*

Special Appendix III: Urban Legends: The Star System

A friend of this project and a major force in the debunking universe is Don L. F. Nilsen of Arizona State University, who has come up with a rating system that affixes stars to the most popular urban legends. Nilsen's gourmet approach to this matter is most refreshing, and we publish the list here as a public service.

Two Stars:
The Alligators in the Sewers
The Baby on the Roof
The Bosom Serpent
The Fifty-Dollar Thunderbird

Three Stars:
The Attempted Abduction
The Corpse in the Cask
The Dog in the Oven
The Nude in the Camper
The Second Blue Book
The Snake in the K Mart

Four Stars:
The Baby and the Turkey
The Bump in the Rug
The Cat and the Salmon
The Clever Baby-Sitter
The Death of Little Mikey
The Elephant That Sat on a VW
The Finger in the Dog's Throat
The Jogger in the Freezer
The Loving but Cold Hand
The Matron's TV
The Mickey Mouse Acid
The Mutilated Boy
The Nude Housewife
The Philanderer's Porsche
The Poison Dress
The Severed Hand
The Stolen Specimen

Five Stars:
The Hairy-Armed Hitchhiker
The Runaway Grandmother
The Ski Accident

Six Stars:
The Manhattan White
The Note from the Witness
The Phantom Hitchhiker
The Purse in the Changing Room
The Strange Gas-Station Attendant

Seven Stars:
The Boyfriend's Death
The Maniac's Hook
The Solid Cement Cadillac

Eight Stars:
The Stuck Couple

THANKS

A number of stalwart credo collectors have contributed their own findings to this work, and we thank them for their generosity. The discoveries of the following people, often in their own words, are spread throughout the book:

David Almasi
John Anders
Ryan Anthony
Brett J. S. Balon
Utica Thomas Banta
Edmund F. Bard
Bob Barnett
Harriet and David Bernstein
Art Berwick
Walter Blair
Murray Teigh Bloom
Carl Bode
Dallas Brozik
Frank Brusca
Richard Cheyney
Nonnee Coan
Bob Cochran
Ed Cocke
Mark B. Cohen
Virginia Cressey
Don Crinklaw
James J. Crowe
James Davis
Robert L. Davis
John W. Dengler
Rose DeWolf
Nancy Dickson
Laura Durst
Lynn Eden

R. K. Edson
Wayne C. Fields, Jr.
Marguerite Foster
Bill Gerk
Kathleen A. Gilbert, of
    Procter & Gamble
Thomas E. Gill
Gary Goettling
Jim Goulden
Trey Goulden
A. C. Greene
John Greenya
Steve Harvey
M. B. Helms
Jim Hely
William D. Hickman
Aesa Hitchens
Charles Holmes
Dave Howard
Terri Hundley
Ed Huser
Michael G. Hutsko
Reed Irvine
Skip Isaacs
Bobbi Kadesch
Joan C. Kaye
Bill Kelly
Robert F. Kendall
Don King

William M. Kipp
F. A. Knaus
Gary M. Knowlton
Lois Kobb
Martin S. Kottmeyer
Lois Landis Kurowski
Richard Lederer
W. D. Lehman
Bob Levey
Arthur H. Lewis
Pete McAlevey
J. Marshall Magner
Peter T. Maiken
Charles Maranto
Maurice Marsolais
Paula Matzek
Henry Morgan
Charles Moss
Russell Mott
Don L. F. Nilsen
Robert Norrish
Andrew J. Novotney, S.J.
Patrick O'Connor
Roger Pitsinger
Judith Podell
Charles D. Poe
Larry Pratt
Frank S. Preston
Randy Randall
Peg Ransom, of The
  Kitchens of Sara Lee
Dan Rapoport

Ross Reader
Admiral Hyman G. Rickover
Vic Ridgley
Ken Rigsbee
Margaret Rubega
Sam Sass
Sandy Schuart
W. N. Scott
Sam Sharkey
W. R. C. Shedenhelm
R. J. Shipley
Bob Skole
Larry M. Slavens
Blane Smith
Jack Smith
Leslie Cantrell Smith
Lindsay Smith
Virgil Smith
Robert D. Specht
Michael A. Stackpole
Norman D. Stevens
Robert A. Sweeney
Bill Tammeus
Craig Tovey
Jamie Tovey
Elaine Viets
Jerry Wall
Greg Walter
John Edward Weems
Rozanne Weissman
Robert H. Yoakum
X. Zeng

BIBLIOGRAPHY

Adams, Cecil. *The Straight Dope.* New York: Ballantine Books, 1984.

Allport, Gordon W., and Leo Postman. *The Psychology of Rumor.* New York: Henry Holt and Company, 1947.

American Academy of Ophthalmology. *Facts and Myths.* San Francisco, 1992 (pamphlet published by the Academy).

Anders, John. "We Hold These Truths to Be Self-evident Bromides." *The Dallas Morning News,* June 12, 1979.

Baker, Ronald L. "The Influence of Mass Culture on Modern Legends." *Southern Folklore Quarterly* 40 (1979), pp. 367–76.

Barry, Edward. "A Word to the Wise: What You 'Know' Can Hurt You, Too." *Chicago Tribune,* December 20, 1960.

Bennett, William J. "Simple Truths." *Newsweek,* January 7, 1980.

Blair, Walter, and Hamlin Hill. *America's Humor: From Poor Richard to Doonesbury.* New York: Oxford University Press, 1978.

Boller, Paul F., Jr. *Presidential Anecdotes.* New York: Oxford University Press, 1981.

Brunvand, Jan Harold. *The Choking Doberman and Other "New" Urban Legends.* New York: W. W. Norton, 1984.

———. *Curses! Boiled Again! The Hottest Urban Legends Going.* New York: W. W. Norton, 1989.

———. *The Study of American Folklore: An Introduction.* New York: W. W. Norton, 1968.

———. *The Vanishing Hitchhiker: American Urban Legends and Their Meanings.* New York: W. W. Norton, 1981.

Burnam, Tom. *The Dictionary of Misinformation.* New York: Thomas Y. Crowell Co., 1975.

———. *More Misinformation.* New York: Lippincott and Crowell, 1980.

Caldwell, Otis W., and Gerbard E. Lundeen. *Do You Believe It? Curious Habits and Strange Beliefs of Civilized Man.* Garden City: Garden City Publishing Co., Inc., 1937.

Camp, John. *Magic, Myth and Medicine.* New York: Taplinger, 1973.

Castle, Sue. *Old Wives' Tales.* New York: Citadel Press, 1992.

Chase, Stuart. *American Credos.* New York: Harper and Brothers, 1962.

Chaundler, Christine. *Every Man's Book of Superstitions*. New York: Philosophical Library, 1970.

Coffin, Tristram Potter. *A Proper Book of Sexual Folklore*. New York: Seabury Press, 1978.

Cohen, Daniel. *Southern Fried Rat, and Other Gruesome Tales*. New York: Avon, 1989.

Curvin, Robert. "Sit!" *The New York Times*, January 7, 1982.

Daley, Robert. *World Beneath the City*. Philadelphia: Lippincott, 1959.

DeWolf, Rose. "Would You Believe Some of the Things We Believe?" *The Bulletin* (Philadelphia), April 30, 1980.

Dickson, Paul and Joseph C. Goulden. *There Are Alligators in Our Sewers: And Other American Credos*. New York: Delacorte, 1983.

Donald, Graeme. *Things You Thought You Thought You Knew!* London: Unwin Paperbacks, 1986.

Dorson, Richard M. *America in Legend*. New York: Pantheon, 1973.

———. *American Folklore*. Chicago: The University of Chicago Press, 1959.

———. *Land of the Millrats*. Cambridge: Harvard University Press, 1981.

Ellul, Jacques. *A Critique of the New Commonplaces*. New York: Alfred A. Knopf, 1968.

Emrich, Duncan. *Folklore on the Land*. Boston: Little, Brown, 1972.

Evans, Bergen. *The Natural History of Nonsense*. New York: Alfred A. Knopf, 1953.

———. *A Spoor of Spooks*. New York: Alfred A. Knopf, 1954.

Ferm, Vergilius. *A Brief Dictionary of American Superstitions*. New York: Philosophical Library, 1965.

Flaubert, Gustave. *The Dictionary of Accepted Ideas*. Translated and with an introduction by Jacques Barzun. New York: New Directions, 1954.

Fowler, Will. *The Second Handshake*. Secaucus, NJ: Lyle Stuart, Inc., 1980.

Gillins, Peter. "Have You Heard About the Mouse in the Pop Bottle?" UPI story in the *Montgomery Journal*, February 3, 1982.

Gold, Bill. "The District Line." *The Washington Post*, March 30, 1979.

Groner, Jonathan. "The Neatness of Myths." *The Washington Post*, April 1, 1979.

Haas, Alan D. "Rumors." *Sunday World-Herald, Magazine of the Midlands*, August 17, 1980.

Harris, James. "An American Credo for the 1980s." *The New Libertarian,* June 1985.

Hering, Daniel W. *Foibles and Fallacies of Science.* New York: Van Nostrand, 1924.

Higgins, George W. "A Little Fantasy for Your Health." *Boston Globe,* August 19, 1981.

Hobson, Thayer. *Morrow's Almanack and Every-Day-Book for 1930.* New York: William Morrow and Co., 1929.

Knapp, Mary and Herbert. *One Potato, Two Potato . . . The Secret Education of American Children.* New York: Norton, 1976.

Lapham, Lewis H. "Program Notes." *Harper's,* May 1979.

Leccese, Michael. "Looking for Mr. Dillinger." *Washington Tribune,* April 1980.

Maddry, Lawrence. "Local Credos: Believe it or Not!" *Virginian-Pilot and the Ledger,* January 30, 1983.

Mansfield, Stephanie. "The Man in the Moon." *The Washington Post,* January 23, 1982.

Molleson, John. "The Explosive Power of Rumors." *Parade,* May 19, 1968.

Montagu, Ashley, and Edward Darling. *The Ignorance of Certainty.* New York: Harper and Row, 1970.

―――. *The Prevalence of Nonsense.* New York: Harper and Row, 1967.

Morris, Scot. "Pssssssst! Have you heard . . . ?" *Omni,* July 1981.

Nathan, George Jean. *The New American Credo.* New York: Blue Ribbon Books, 1927.

Nathan, George Jean, and H. L. Mencken. *The American Credo.* New York; Alfred A. Knopf, 1920.

Nilsen, Don L. F. "Contemporary Legend: The Definition of a Genre." *Kansas English* 75.1 (1989): 5–10.

Oberg, James. "Spaceflight Folklore." *Analog,* September 1980.

Opie, Iona and Peter. *The Lore and Language of Schoolchildren.* Oxford: Oxford Press, 1959.

Palmer, Barbara. "Myths of Washington." *The Washingtonian,* January 1980.

Poundstone, William. *Big Secrets.* New York: William Morrow, 1983.

"Procter & Gamble Is Clean." *Newsweek,* April 7, 1980.

Rosten, Leo. *The Power of Positive Nonsense.* New York: McGraw-Hill, 1977.

Runes, Dagoburt D. *Dictionary of Thought.* New York: Philosophical Library, 1959.

Sarnoff, Jane, and Reunold Ruins. *Take Warning! A Book of Superstitions.* New York: Scribner's, 1978.

Smith, Jack. "In a New Collection of Repeated Yarns, Authors Lay Their Cards on the Table." *Los Angeles Times,* September 1, 1983.

Smith, Paul. *The Book of Nastier Legends.* New York: Routledge and Kegan Paul, 1986.

———. *The Book of Nasty Legends.* New York: Routledge and Kegan Paul, 1983.

———. *Perspectives on Contemporary Legend.* Sheffield, England: Centre for English Cultural Tradition and Language, 1984.

"The Great Fables of Our Time." *Oui,* September 1976.

"The Hell with the Donuts." *The DAV Magazine,* April 1961.

Viets, Elaine. "If There's One Thing for Certain, It's That . . ." *St. Louis Post-Dispatch,* July 1, 1979.

Ward, Philip. *Dictionary of Common Fallacies.* New York: Oleander Press, 1978.

Weinstein, Jeff. "Four Lies About Gay Male Fashion." *The Village Voice,* April 8–14, 1981.

Welsch, Roger. *Shingling the Fog, and Other Plains Lies.* Lincoln: University of Nebraska Press, 1972.

Werwein, Austin C. "Logo Rumors Haunt P&G." *The Washington Post,* March 26, 1980.

West, Woody. "How the Public Was Snake-Bitten by a Rumor." Washington *Star,* February 23, 1969.

Wiggam, Albert Edward. *The Marks of a Clear Mind.* New York: Blue Ribbon Books, Inc., 1931.

Wingate, P. J. *H. L. Mencken's Un-Neglected Anniversary.* Hockessin, DE: The Holly Press, 1980.

INDEX

ABOUT THE AUTHOR

Paul Dickson has written more than thirty books and over three hundred magazine articles. His books have concentrated on such far-flung subjects as toys, think tanks, working conditions, baseball, the American language, and ice cream. *The Dickson Baseball Dictionary* won several national awards, including the SABR-Macmillan Baseball Research Award. He lives in Garrett Park, Maryland, and is a contributing editor to *Washingtonian* magazine.

Joseph C. Goulden, a native of Marshall, Texas, began his newspaper career with the Marshall *News-Messenger* and later reported for the *Dallas Morning News* and the *Philadelphia Inquirer,* lastly as Washington bureau chief. He is a founder of the H. L. Mencken Society and Washington Independent Writers and a member of the Association of Former Intelligence Officers. The author of sixteen nonfiction books, including several national bestsellers, he is director of media analysis for Accuracy in Media, a Washington-based press watchdog group. He lives in Georgetown with his wife, Leslie Cantrell Smith.